Simple Appeal

Simple Appeal

14 Patchwork and Appliqué Projects for Everyday Living

Kim Diehl

Martingale®
Create with Confidence

Acknowledgments

To Deb Behrend, Pat Peyton, and Barbara Walsh, a big thank-you to each of you for your excellent piecing skills and outstanding workmanship on my projects, and most of all, for being such wonderful quilting friends.

My sincerest thanks to the quilting staff at The Gathering Place in Rupert, Idaho, and especially to my own personal quilting goddess, Deborah Poole, for your beautiful machine quilting—your stitching skills are completely divine and always give my projects the perfect finish.

A huge thank-you to Laurie Baker for your technical expertise, wicked wit, and continued friendship as we tackle each new book project. . . . I bow to your knowledge, oh wise one!

My ongoing appreciation and thanks to the entire Martingale team for your creativity and standards of excellence in helping me grow the seeds of an idea into this finished book.

Many thanks to Janome America for the amazing Memory Craft 11000 sewing machine that makes piecing and appliquéing my quilts such a joy.

And as always, a big thank-you to Jo Morton for the bundles of your beautiful fabrics that I love to mingle with my own Henry Glass prints when I stitch my quilts.

Simple Appeal: 14 Patchwork and
Appliqué Projects for Everyday Living
© 2014 by Kim Diehl

Martingale®
19021 120th Ave. NE, Ste. 102
Bothell, WA 98011-5511 USA
ShopMartingale.com

Printed in China
19 18 17 16 15 14   8 7 6 5 4 3 2 1

Library of Congress Cataloging-in-Publication Data is available upon request.

ISBN: 978-1-60468-297-7

Mission Statement
Dedicated to providing quality products and service to inspire creativity.

Credits
PRESIDENT AND CEO: Tom Wierzbicki
EDITOR IN CHIEF: Mary V. Green
DESIGN DIRECTOR: Paula Schlosser
MANAGING EDITOR: Karen Costello Soltys
ACQUISITIONS EDITOR: Karen M. Burns
TECHNICAL EDITOR: Laurie Baker
COPY EDITOR: Melissa Bryan
PRODUCTION MANAGER: Regina Girard
COVER DESIGNER: Paula Schlosser
INTERIOR DESIGNER: Regina Girard
PHOTOGRAPHER: Brent Kane
ILLUSTRATOR: Missy Shepler

Special thanks to Sheila and Jonathan Waterman of Duvall, Washington, for graciously allowing us to photograph in their home.

Contents

Introduction

From the time I was a little girl, I've been blessed to have quilts in my life. Not fancy quilts, not exquisitely sewn works of art, just everyday quilts stitched with love by my grandmother.

Quilts can mean many different things to many different people. To me, seeing how my grandma sometimes stitched together the tiniest pieces of cloth from flour sacks, dresses, and blouses, just to be able to make her quilts and fashion something beautiful while keeping her family warm, this is the true appeal and meaning of a quilt. My very favorite quilts, and the quilts I continue to make to this day, are rooted in this rich tradition that's been passed on from generation to generation, or in my case, from grandmother to granddaughter.

In the spirit of my grandma's "no nonsense" quiltmaking approach, and also with the goal of being able to put a myriad of different scraps and bits and pieces to good use, many of the projects in this collection are fat-quarter and fat-eighth friendly—you can easily raid your stash and scraps for a bit of instant gratification. You'll also find that the quilts and projects in this collection incorporate tried-and-true blocks and motifs that have long been treasured by quiltmakers; none are fussy or fancy, and all are comfy and inviting. Best of all, the methods used to make these traditional quilts include modern timesaving techniques and richly hued color schemes. What a perfect blend of old and new!

I've always felt that the appeal of quilts intended for everyday living is that they lend a welcoming air to any room and instantly make your house feel like a home; they're meant to be lived with, wrapped up in, and enjoyed for many years to come. It's my hope as you look through the pages of this book that you'll be inspired to share your own unique creativity and generosity of spirit, and bring a smile to the face of someone you love through the most priceless of gifts . . . the gift of a quilt.

Sprigs and Twigs

*P*luck an armful of your favorite richly hued prints, cut them into twig-like strips, and stitch a crop of these simply sewn patchwork blocks. Surround your scrappy garden with sprigs of gently meandering appliqués, and reap what you sew for many seasons to come.

Materials

32 fat eighths (9" x 22") of assorted prints for blocks and flower appliqués*

1⅞ yards of black print for outer border

1 yard of red print for block and flower-center nine-patch units, inner-border corner squares, berry appliqués, and binding

¾ yard of green stripe for vine, stem, and leaf appliqués

⅔ yard of tan print for block and flower-center nine-patch units, and inner border

2 fat eighths of assorted coordinating green prints for leaf appliqués

4 yards of fabric for backing

67" x 67" square of batting

Bias bar to fit your stems and vines

Appliqué supplies (see page 99)

If you wish to use fewer prints, you can substitute 16 fat quarters measuring 18" x 22".

Cutting

Cut all pieces across the width of the fabric in the order given unless otherwise noted. Refer to page 15 for appliqué patterns A–F and to "Invisible Machine Appliqué" beginning on page 99 for pattern piece preparation. Refer to "Cutting Bias Strips" on page 96 to cut bias strips.

From the tan print, cut:
13 strips, 1½" x 42"

From the red print, cut:
5 strips, 1½" x 42"; crosscut *1 of the strips* into 4 squares, 1½" x 1½". Reserve the remaining strips for the strip-pieced nine-patch units.
7 binding strips, 2½" x 42"
54 berry appliqués using pattern F

From the 32 assorted print fat eighths, cut a *combined total* of:
32 rectangles, 1½" x 3½" (A)
64 rectangles, 1½" x 5½" (B)
64 rectangles, 1½" x 7½" (C)
64 rectangles, 1½" x 9½" (D)
32 rectangles, 1½" x 11½" (E)
4 large flower appliqués using pattern A
14 small flower appliqués using pattern B
14 small flower center appliqués using pattern C

From the *bias* of the green stripe, cut:
Enough 1¼"-wide strips to make two lengths measuring 50" each when pieced together end to end using straight, not diagonal, seams
4 strips, 1¼" x 24"
12 strips, 1¼" x 4½"

From the remainder of the green stripe, cut:
13 leaf appliqués using pattern E

From the *lengthwise grain* of the black print, cut:
2 strips, 7½" x 46½"
2 strips, 7½" x 60½"

From the green print fat eighths, cut a *combined total* of:
25 leaf appliqués using pattern E

"Sprigs and Twigs"

FINISHED QUILT SIZE: 60½" x 60½"

FINISHED BLOCK SIZE: 11" x 11"

Designed, pieced, and machine appliquéd by Kim Diehl. Machine quilted by Deborah Poole.

Piecing the Blocks

Sew all pieces with right sides together using a ¼" seam allowance unless otherwise noted.

1. Join two tan 1½" x 42" strips and one red 1½" x 42" strip along the long edges as shown to make strip set A. Press the seam allowances toward the red strip. Repeat for a total of two strip sets. Crosscut the strip sets into 40 segments, 1½" wide.

Strip set A.
Make 2. Cut 40 segments.

2. Join two red 1½" x 42" strips and one tan 1½" x 42" strip along the long edges as shown to make strip set B. Press the seam allowances toward the red strips. Crosscut the strip set into 20 segments, 1½" wide.

Strip set B.
Make 1. Cut 20 segments.

3. Lay out two A segments and one B segment in three horizontal rows as shown to form a nine patch. Join the rows. Press the seam allowances toward the middle row. Repeat for a total of 20 nine-patch units.

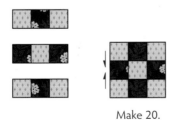

Make 20.

4. Join two assorted print A rectangles to opposite sides of a nine-patch unit from step 3. Press the seam allowances toward the rectangles. In the same manner, join and press two B rectangles to the remaining sides of the nine-patch unit. Referring to the illustration, continue building

and stitching the block, working from the shortest to the longest rectangles. Repeat for a total of 16 pieced blocks measuring 11½" square, including the seam allowances. Reserve the remaining nine-patch units for later use.

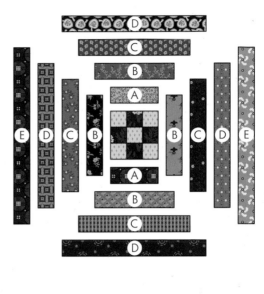

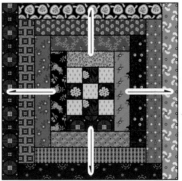

Make 16.

Piecing the Quilt Center and Inner Border

1. Lay out four pieced blocks, turning every other block as shown so that the A rectangles rotate between the top and bottom and the sides. Join the blocks to make a pieced row. Press the seam allowances toward the block edges with no seams. Repeat for a total of four pieced rows. Join the rows. Press the seam allowances open. The pieced quilt center should now measure 44½" square, including the seam allowances.

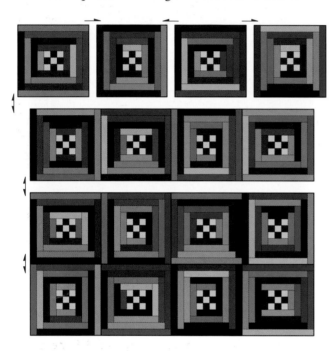

2. Join two tan 1½" x 42" strips end to end. Press the seam allowances open. Repeat for a total of four pieced strips. For each strip, measure 22¼" outward from each side of the center seam and use a rotary cutter and acrylic ruler to trim away the ends; the trimmed strips should now measure 44½" in length.

22¼"   22¼"

Make 4.

3. Join pieced tan strips from step 2 to the right and left sides of the quilt center. Press the seam allowances toward the tan strips. Join a red 1½" square to each end of the remaining pieced tan strips. Press the seam allowances toward the tan strips. Join these strips to the remaining sides of the quilt center. Press the seam allowances toward the tan strips. The quilt top should now measure 46½" square, including the seam allowances.

Appliquéing and Adding the Outer Border

1. Join the green stripe 1¼"-wide lengths end to end to make a pieced 50" strip using straight, not diagonal, seams. Repeat for a total of two pieced strips. Referring to "Making Bias-Tube Stems and Vines" on page 102, prepare the 50" vines, the 24" vines, and the 4½" stems.

2. Referring to "Preparing Paper Pattern Pieces" on page 100 and using pattern D on page 15, cut four circles from freezer paper. Referring to "Preparing Appliqués" on page 100, center and affix a freezer-paper circle to the wrong side of a reserved nine-patch unit; prepare the appliqué for stitching, leaving a generous ¼" seam allowance to enable the nine-patch seams to remain firmly in place after the edges have been turned to the back of the appliqué. Repeat for a total of four prepared nine-patch flower-center appliqués.

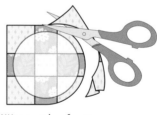

Wrong side of unit

3. Referring to "Preparing Appliqués," prepare the appliqués for stitching. (Before proceeding with the remaining border appliqué steps, you may wish to lay out the black 46½" and 60½" strips along the pieced quilt-center edges to ensure that no size adjustments are needed and that they will fit properly.)

4. Using the quilt photo on page 10 as a guide, lay out a prepared 50" vine onto a 46½" side border strip, allowing an extra 3" to 4" of length to extend beyond the end where the vine will later adjoin with the large corner flower; when you're happy with the placement of the vine, place tiny dots of liquid basting glue at approximately ½" to 1" intervals on the underside of the vine to anchor it in place. Next, glue baste four prepared 4½" stems along the vine, tucking the raw ends well to the center of the vine to prevent fraying. Last, position and glue baste nine prepared leaves along the vine. Heat set the vine, stems, and leaves from the back of the strip. Referring to "Stitching Appliqués" on page 104 and "Removing Paper Pattern Pieces" on pages 105 and 106, stitch the vine, stem, and leaf appliqués in place and then remove the pattern pieces. Work from the bottom layer to the top to lay out, glue baste, and stitch three small flowers, three small flower centers, and 15 berries, remembering to remove the paper pattern pieces before adding each new layer. Pin the excess length of vine away from the strip end to keep it from being stitched into the seam when the appliquéd strip is joined to the quilt center. Repeat with the remaining 46½" border strip.

PIN POINT

Plump Stems and Vines

After preparing my stems and vines for an appliqué project and glue basting the seam allowances, I've noticed that some stems can have a flat appearance because the top layer of fabric has become slightly adhered to the seam after heat setting. When this occurs, I simply pop my bias bar back into the stem and slide it through the layers to separate the cloth. Taking a moment to do this quick step will result in plump stems and vines that will really make your appliqué design shine.

5. Using the quilt photo as a guide, position a large flower appliqué onto each end of a black 60½" top/bottom border strip; pin in place. Lay out a prepared 24" vine on each end of the strip, tucking the raw ends under the flowers at least ¼". When you're happy with the placement of the vines, glue baste them as previously instructed. Next, glue baste and add a prepared 4½" stem to each vine. Last, position and glue baste five prepared leaves along each vine. Remove the large flowers. Heat set the vines, stems, and leaves from the back of the strips. Stitch the appliqués and remove the paper pattern pieces. Work from the bottom layer to the top to reposition and glue baste one large flower, two small flowers, two small flower centers, and six berries along each vine, remembering to remove the paper pattern pieces before adding each new layer. When stitching the large flowers, leave the bottom half of each appliqué unstitched with the paper pattern piece intact to enable you to add the end of the side-border vines after the side borders have been joined to the quilt center. Repeat for a total of two appliquéd 60½" strips.

6. Referring to the quilt photo, join appliquéd 46½" strips to the right and left sides of the quilt center. Press the seam allowances away from the appliquéd strips, taking care not to apply heat to the appliqués. Join the 60½" appliquéd strips to the remaining sides of the quilt center. Press the seam allowances away from the appliquéd strips. Next, unpin the vines on the side borders. Position and glue baste these vines with the raw ends positioned under the large flowers; stitch in place. Finish stitching the large flower appliqués and remove the paper pattern pieces. Last, position, glue baste, and stitch a nine-patch flower center to each large flower; remove the paper pattern pieces. The pieced and appliquéd quilt top should now measure 60½" square, including the seam allowances.

Completing the Quilt

Referring to "Finishing Techniques" on page 108 for any details needed, layer the quilt top, batting, and backing. Quilt the layers. The featured quilt was machine quilted with cross-hatching placed onto the nine-patch units in the blocks and large flower centers. Cross-hatching and cable quilting designs were stitched onto the block rows, with the designs alternating to fill the blocks. An egg-and-dart design was stitched onto the inner border, and the outer border was echo quilted to emphasize the appliqué design. Join the seven red 2½" x 42" strips into one length and use it to bind the quilt.

PIN POINT

Easily Organized Fat Quarters

Because my sewing room is so small and space is at a premium, I've worked hard to find creative ways to stay organized. One of my favorite repurposed storage items has been a clear plastic over-the-door shoe organizer (found in the home section of most department stores) to help keep my fat quarter and fat eighth prints within easy reach and enable me to see at a glance what's available. I roll these fabric pieces up into little bundles to fit the plastic cubbies and sort them by color—it makes choosing prints for my new projects a snap. Love this little trick!

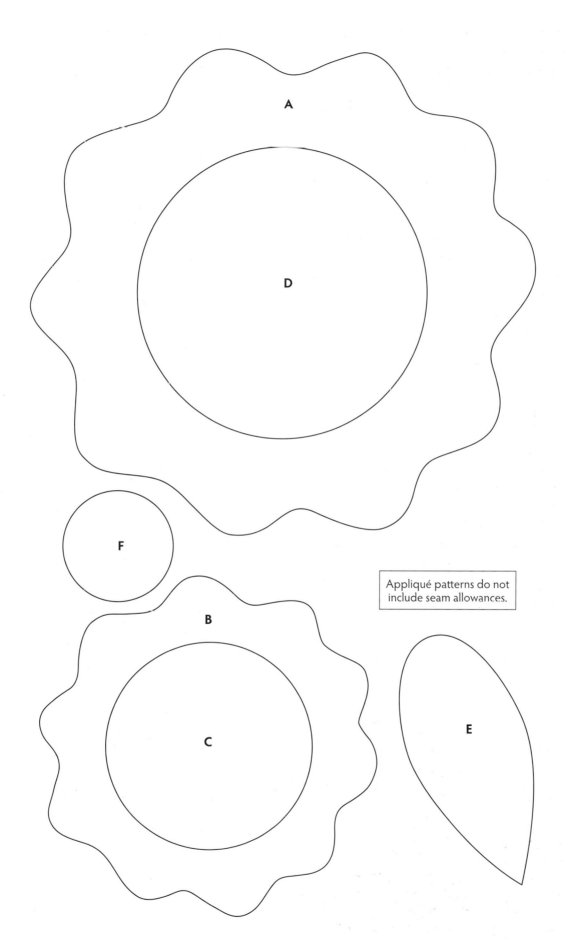

A

D

F

B

C

Appliqué patterns do not
include seam allowances.

E

Penny Garland

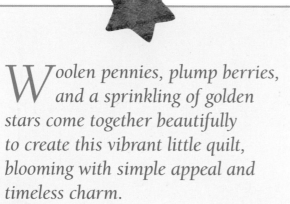

W oolen pennies, plump berries, and a sprinkling of golden stars come together beautifully to create this vibrant little quilt, blooming with simple appeal and timeless charm.

Materials

1 yard of light-tan print for background

½ yard of chocolate-brown print for vine and binding

20 rectangles, 6" x 10", of assorted wools for pennies and layered ovals*

4 rectangles, 6" x 10", of assorted green wools for leaves

4 squares, 6" x 6", of assorted gold wools for stars

4 squares, 4" x 4", of assorted red wools for berries

1 yard of fabric for backing

36" x 36" square of batting

Bias bar to fit your vine

Approximately 2 yards of HeatnBond Lite iron-on adhesive

1 spool of #8 or #12 perle cotton (I used Valdani's #12 variegated perle cotton in H212 Faded Brown)

Size 5 embroidery needle

Fine-tip water-soluble marker

Appliqué supplies (see page 106)

*For a super-scrappy look like the pictured project, you can substitute an assortment of wool scraps, 4" square and smaller.

Cutting

Cut all pieces across the width of the fabric in the order given unless otherwise noted. Refer to page 21 for appliqué patterns A–G and to "Wool Appliqué" beginning on page 106 for pattern piece preparation. Refer to "Cutting Bias Strips" on page 96 to cut bias strips.

From the light-tan print, cut:

1 square, 30½" x 30½"

From the chocolate-brown print, cut:

3 binding strips, 2½" x 42"

From the *bias* of the remainder of the chocolate-brown print, cut:

Enough 1¼"-wide strips to make a 64" length when pieced together end to end using straight, not diagonal, seams

From the 6" x 10" rectangles of assorted wools, cut a *combined total* of:

9 large penny circles using pattern A

9 medium penny circles using pattern B

9 small penny circles using pattern C

32 large ovals using pattern D

32 small ovals using pattern E

From the 6" x 10" rectangles of assorted green wools, cut a *combined total* of:

24 leaves using pattern F

From the 6" x 6" squares of assorted gold wools, cut a *combined total* of:

16 stars using pattern G

From the 4" x 4" squares of assorted red wools, cut a *combined total* of:

16 berries using pattern C

"Penny Garland"

FINISHED QUILT SIZE: 30½" x 30½"

Designed and hand appliquéd by Kim Diehl.
Machine quilted by Deborah Poole, with hand-quilting accents by Kim Diehl.

Preparing the Quilt Background

1. Fold the tan 30½" square in half, right sides together, and use a hot, dry iron to press a center vertical crease. Refold and press to add a center horizontal crease.

2. Measure 6¾" outward from each side of the center creases along the quilt edges; use the water-soluble marker to mark these points.

3. Use the water-soluble marker and an acrylic ruler to draw a diagonal line across each corner of the square to connect the marked dots. These lines will outline the unused portions of the square; you'll trim away the excess fabric after the appliqué is complete.

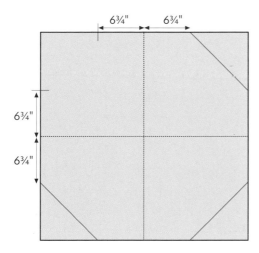

4. Using an acrylic ruler, measure 3¼" in from each vertical and horizontal edge of the tan square and lightly draw a line with the water-soluble marker. Repeat with each corner of the square, measuring 3¼" in from the previously drawn diagonal lines and extending these lines to intersect with the vertical and horizontal lines. This will outline the area where the oval wool pieces will be positioned.

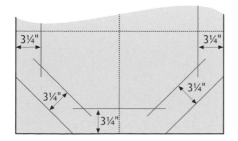

5. Referring to "Preparing Pattern Templates" on page 100, make a template of the large penny

circle A pattern on page 21. Fold the template circle in half and finger-press a center vertical crease. Refold to press a second horizontal crease.

Round Items for Tracing

I've found that circles can be really challenging to trace accurately from pattern sheets, so I look for and collect round things of all different sizes to keep on hand in my circle "template" collection. Buttons, spools, coins, lids, tape rolls, washers, even Life Savers are fair game and can be the perfect match for a circle shape needed for an appliqué project. Tracing around the raised edges of these items is infinitely easier than tracing over curved lines on a pattern sheet, so consider starting a collection of your own, and simplify your appliqué preparation steps.

6. Position the prepared circle template onto the tan square, aligning the template creases with the fabric creases to perfectly center it. Use the water-soluble marker to trace around the edge of the circle. This traced circle will enable you to easily center and position the pennies when you begin to build your design.

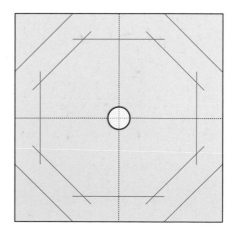

Preparing the Vine

Join the brown 1¼"-wide bias strips end to end to make a 64" length, using straight, not diagonal, seams. Referring to "Making Bias-Tube Stems and Vines" on page 102, prepare the vine.

Laying Out the Appliqué Design

1. Referring to "Wool Appliqué," prepare, layer, glue baste, heat set, and stitch nine stacked wool penny units using the A, B, and C appliqués. Remove the paper backing from the bottom-most penny of each stitched unit, and apply small dots of liquid basting glue onto the rim of adhesive. Place one prepared penny stack onto the tan print square, positioning it onto the drawn circle to perfectly center it.

2. Referring to the quilt photo on page 18, continue positioning penny stacks around the center penny unit with the edges just touching. If the traced line around the center circle is visible once the penny stacks are in place, carefully blot it away with a piece of wet muslin or a white paper towel. Use a hot, dry iron to heat set the penny units from the back of your work. Stitch the penny stacks to the background.

3. Referring to the quilt photo, lay out the vine in the center area between the wool pennies and the drawn straight lines where the wool ovals will be positioned. (Keep in mind as you establish your vine curves that you'll be adding leaves, stars, and berries, and your design should be positioned with enough room to add these pieces without placing them within the drawn margin around the quilt edge.) Begin your vine placement at an outer curve, anchoring the shape loosely with straight pins to establish the design. When you're pleased with the shape, apply small dots of glue to the underside of the vine at approximately ½" intervals to anchor it in place, fine-tuning and smoothing the curves as you progress. When you reach your starting point, trim away any excess stem length and ensure the raw vine ends rest together. Heat set the vine from the back of your work. Use your favorite appliqué method to stitch the vine in place. (The vine in the featured quilt was hand stitched using a size 9 straw needle and matching brown thread.)

4. Using the quilt photo as a guide, lay out, glue baste, and heat set the leaves along the vine, add the stars, and then finish with the berries. Please note that I positioned a handful of berries on top of the stem, ensuring that one berry covered the raw ends of the vine. Stitch each of the wool appliqués in place.

5. Prepare and stitch together 32 layered wool oval units as previously instructed. Remove the paper backing strip from the bottom of each prepared oval unit and apply small dots of glue to the adhesive. Position four prepared oval units along each straight edge of the tan print square, using the center background creases to achieve even placement and aligning the straight edges with the raw edges of the square. Repeat with the diagonal sides of the quilt, positioning the remaining ovals onto the outer drawn lines at the corners of the background square. When you're pleased with your placement, heat set the ovals from the back of your work, and stitch them in place.

Completing the Quilt

1. Referring to "Finishing Techniques" on page 108, layer the quilt top, batting, and backing.

2. Quilt the layers. The featured project was machine quilted with an echo quilt design over the entire background area. The appliqués were outline quilted in the big-stitch method using perle cotton (see "Big-Stitch Quilting" on page 109).

3. Use an acrylic ruler and a rotary cutter to trim away the outer corners of the tan square, cutting exactly on the drawn diagonal lines.

4. Join the three brown 2½" x 42" strips into one length and use it to bind the quilt.

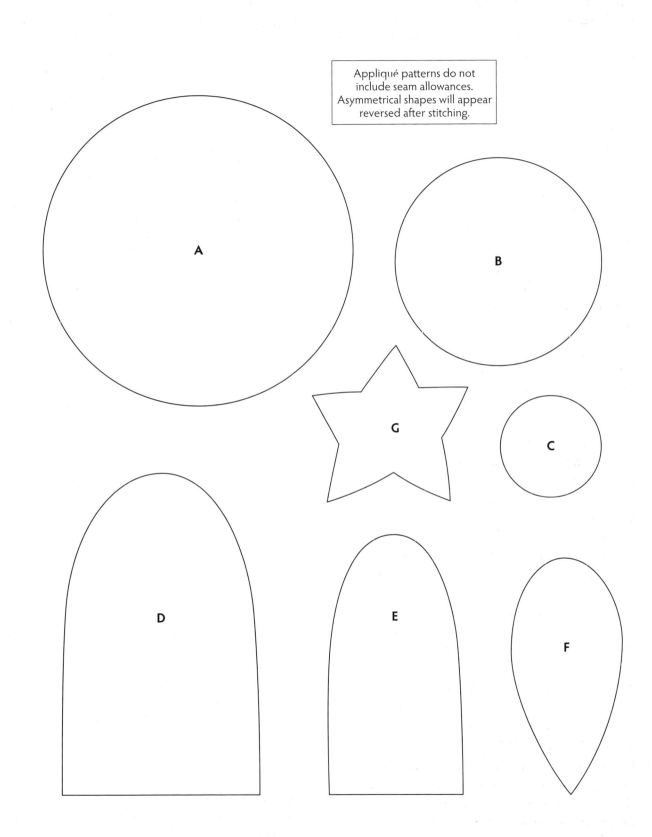

Appliqué patterns do not
include seam allowances.
Asymmetrical shapes will appear
reversed after stitching.

A

B

G

C

D

E

F

Esther's Baskets

Tradition abounds with these tiny crimson baskets, exuding time-honored elegance in a classic color scheme long favored by quiltmakers. For a bit of "make-do" flair, take a different approach: raid your scrap basket, and fashion your blocks from a rainbow of leftover prints.

FINISHED QUILT SIZE: 13½" x 13½"

FINISHED BLOCK SIZE: 3" x 3"

Designed, pieced, and hand appliquéd by Kim Diehl. Machine quilted by Deborah Poole.

Materials

8 chubby sixteenths (9" x 11") of assorted red prints for blocks and binding

1 fat quarter (18" x 22") of red print for blocks and border

2 fat eighths (9" x 22") of assorted cream prints for blocks

1 fat eighth of cream-and-red stripe for border

1 fat quarter of fabric for backing

18" x 18" square of batting

Bias bar to fit your basket handles

Appliqué supplies (see page 99)

Cutting

Cut all pieces across the width of the fabric in the order given unless otherwise noted.

From the fat quarter of red print, cut:
2 strips, 1½" x 13½"
2 strips, 1" x 13½"
1 strip, 1½" x 22"; crosscut into 2 strips, 1½" x 9½"
1 strip, 1" x 22"; crosscut into 2 strips, 1" x 9½"
1 *bias* strip, 1" x 5"
1 rectangle, 1½" x 3½"
1 rectangle, 1" x 2½"

From *each* of the 8 assorted red print chubby sixteenths, cut:
1 rectangle, 1½" x 3½" (combined total of 8)
1 rectangle, 1" x 2½" (combined total of 8)
1 *bias* strip, 1" x 5" (combined total of 8)

From the remainder of the assorted red prints, cut:
Enough 2½"-wide random-length strips to make a 64" length of binding when pieced together end to end using straight, not diagonal, seams

From *1* of the cream prints, cut:
5 rectangles, 2" x 3½"
10 squares, 1½" x 1½"
10 rectangles, 1" x 1½"

From the remaining assorted cream print, cut:
4 rectangles, 2" x 3½"
8 squares, 1½" x 1½"
8 rectangles, 1" x 1½"

From the cream-and-red stripe, cut:
1 strip, 1" x 22"; crosscut into 2 strips, 1" x 9½"
2 strips, 1" x 13½"

Piecing the Blocks

Sew all pieces with right sides together using a ¼" seam allowance unless otherwise noted.

1. Referring to "Making Bias-Tube Stems and Vines" on page 102, prepare each of the red 1" x 5" bias strips for use as basket handles.

2. Apply small dots of liquid basting glue to the seam of a prepared handle. Referring to the quilt photo, position the handle onto a cream 2" x 3½" rectangle with the raw edges flush at the bottom rectangle edge and the outer curve resting approximately ½" in from each side and top edge; trim away any excess handle length. Use your favorite appliqué method to stitch the handle in place. (The basket handles in the featured quilt were hand stitched using a size 9 straw needle and matching red thread.) Repeat with the remaining handles and cream rectangles to make a total of nine basket handle units.

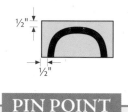

PIN POINT

Consistently Shaped Basket Handles

For uniformly shaped basket handles, I glue basted the first bias handle onto the background rectangle in a way that pleased me, and then placed a 2" x 3½" rectangle of freezer paper with the dull paper side up over the unit, lining up the bottom straight edges. I used a water-soluble marker to trace the inner curve of the handle onto the paper, fused a second rectangle of freezer paper to the traced piece, and then cut along the drawn curved line to make a template. After folding the template in half to finger-press and mark the center position, I folded and finger-pressed each background 2" x 3½" rectangle in half to mark the center, aligned the crease of the template with the background crease (with the bottom straight edges flush), and traced the curve using a water-soluble marker. Last, I dotted each prepared handle with liquid basting glue and used the drawn lines to shape the handles, placing them exactly along the outer curve of the drawn lines. After stitching, any visible lines were blotted away with a wet white paper towel to make them disappear. Quick and easy!

3. Use a pencil and an acrylic ruler to draw a diagonal line from corner to corner on the wrong side of each cream 1½" square.

4. Select one basket handle unit, two matching prepared cream 1½" squares, two matching cream 1" x 1½" rectangles, one matching red 1½" x 3½" rectangle, and one matching red 1" x 2½" rectangle.

5. Layer a cream 1½" square onto each end of the red 1½" x 3½" rectangle as shown. Stitch the squares on the drawn lines. Fold the inner corner of each stitched square open to form the basket unit. Press and trim as instructed in "Pressing Triangle Units" on page 98.

6. Layer a cream 1" x 1½" rectangle onto each side of the red 1" x 2½" rectangle as shown. Use a pencil and an acrylic ruler to draw diagonal stitching lines from the inner top cream corners down to where the outer bottom edges intersect the red print. Stitch the pieces on the drawn lines. Fold

the bottom of the cream rectangles open to form the basket base. Press and trim as instructed in "Pressing Triangle Units."

7. Lay out the basket handle unit, the basket unit, and the basket base. Join the rows. Press the seam allowance of the handle unit toward the basket. Press the seam allowance of the basket base open.

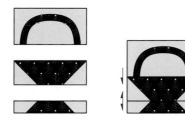

8. Repeat steps 4–7 to make nine pieced Basket blocks measuring 3½" square, including the seam allowances.

Piecing the Quilt Top

1. Refer to the quilt assembly diagram to lay out the Basket blocks in three rows of three blocks each, positioning the five matching blocks in the corners and quilt center. Join the blocks in each horizontal row. Press the seam allowances open. Join the rows. Press the seam allowances away from the basket bases.

2. Join a red 1" x 9½" and 1½" x 9½" strip to each long side of a cream stripe 1" x 9½" strip. Press the seam allowances toward the red strips.

Repeat to make two pieced strips. Join these strips to the right and left sides of the quilt center. Press the seam allowances away from the quilt center. In the same manner, make two pieced strips using the remaining red and cream stripe 13½" strips. Join these pieced strips to the remaining sides of the quilt center. Press the seam allowances away from the quilt center. The pieced quilt top should now measure 13½" square, including the seam allowances.

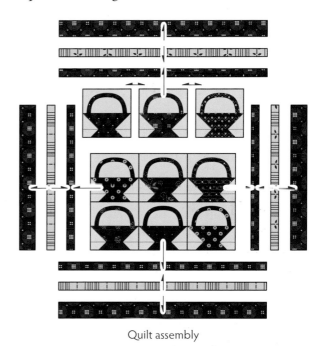

Quilt assembly

Completing the Quilt

Referring to "Finishing Techniques" on page 108, layer the quilt top, batting, and backing. Quilt the layers. Each basket of the featured project was machine quilted with a tiny crosshatch, the block backgrounds were stitched with a micro-stipple, and the background areas between the handle and basket were quilted with small feathered wreath halves. The inner borders were stitched with a crosshatch design, the middle borders were quilted along the lines of the striped print, and a small-scale serpentine feathered vine was stitched onto the outer border. Join the random lengths of red 2½"-wide strips to make a 64" strip and use it to bind the quilt.

*C*ombine classic blocks and motifs with exuberant, colorful prints, toss in a bevy of whimsical flowers, and what's the happy result? This cheerful lap quilt, brimming with modern tradition.

Materials

30 fat quarters (18" x 22") of assorted prints (including some green) for blocks, border, and appliqués

1¾ yards of tan print for background

5 squares, 3½" x 3½", of assorted prints for Star block centers

⅝ yard of black print for binding

4 yards of fabric for backing

72" x 72" square of batting

Bias bar to fit your stem

Appliqué supplies (see page 99)

Cutting

Cut all pieces across the width of fabric in the order given unless otherwise noted. For greater ease in preparation, cutting instructions are provided separately for the appliqués. Refer to "Cutting Bias Strips" on page 96 to cut bias strips.

From the tan print, cut:

4 strips, 9½" x 42"; crosscut *each* strip into:
  1 rectangle, 9½" x 27½" (combined total of 4)
  1 square, 9½" x 9½" (combined total of 4)
10 squares, 4¼" x 4¼"; cut each square in half diagonally *once* to make 20 triangles
20 squares, 3½" x 3½"

From *each* of the 30 assorted print fat quarters, cut:

3 squares, 6¼" x 6¼"; cut each square in half diagonally *once* to make 6 triangles (combined total of 180)

From the remainder of the assorted print fat quarters, cut a *combined total* of:

8 squares, 9½" x 9½"
16 squares, 5¾" x 5¾"; cut each square in half diagonally *once* to make 32 triangles
10 squares, 4¼" x 4¼"; cut each square in half diagonally *once* to make 20 triangles
Reserve the scraps for the appliqués.

From the *bias* of one of the green print fat quarters, cut:

8 strips, 1¼" x 8"
4 strips, 1¼" x 5"
Reserve the scraps for the appliqués.

From the black print, cut:

7 binding strips, 2½" x 42"

Piecing the Star Blocks

Sew all pieces with right sides together using a ¼" seam allowance unless otherwise noted.

1. Layer together an assorted print 4¼" triangle and a tan 4¼" triangle. Stitch the pair together along the long diagonal edges. Press the seam allowances toward the assorted print triangle. Trim away the dog-ear points. Repeat for a total of 20 half-square-triangle units.

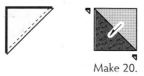

Make 20.

2. Cut each half-square-triangle unit in half as shown to make a total of 40 pieced triangles.

Make 40.

"Late Bloomers"
FINISHED QUILT SIZE: 65½" x 65½"
FINISHED BLOCK SIZE: 9" x 9"
Designed, pieced, and machine appliquéd by Kim Diehl. Machine quilted by Deborah Poole.

3. Select two pieced triangles sewn from different prints. Repeat step 1 to join the pieced triangles. Press the seam allowances to one side. Trim away the dog-ear points. Repeat for a total of 20 small pieced hourglass units measuring 3½" square, including the seam allowances.

Make 20.

4. Lay out four hourglass units, four tan 3½" squares, and one assorted print 3½" square in three horizontal rows as shown to form a Star block. Join the pieces in each row. Press the seam allowances toward the whole squares. Join the rows. Press the seam allowances away from the middle row. Repeat for a total of five pieced Star blocks measuring 9½" square, including the seam allowances.

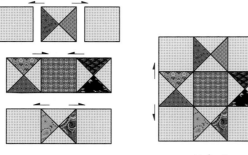

Make 5.

Piecing the Quilt-Center Hourglass Blocks

1. Join two assorted print 5¾" triangles along the long diagonal edges. Press the seam allowances to one side. Trim away the dog-ear points. Repeat for a total of 16 half-square-triangle units.

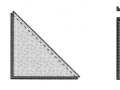

Make 16.

2. Cut each half-square-triangle unit in half as shown to make a total of 32 pieced triangles.

Make 32.

3. Select two pieced triangles sewn from different prints. Repeat step 1 to join the pieced triangles as shown. Press the seam allowances to one side. Trim away the dog-ear points. Repeat for a total of 16 pieced hourglass units measuring 5" square, including the seam allowances.

Make 16.

4. Lay out four hourglass units into two horizontal rows of two units each as shown. Join the pieces in each row. Press the seam allowances of each row in opposite directions. Join the rows. Press the seam allowances open. Repeat for a total of four pieced Hourglass blocks measuring 9½" square, including the seam allowances.

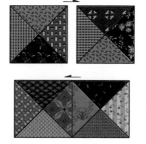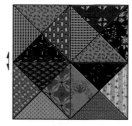

Make 4.

Piecing the Quilt-Center Star Points

1. Use a pencil and an acrylic ruler to draw a diagonal line from corner to corner on the wrong side of each assorted print 9½" square.

2. Layer a prepared 9½" square onto one end of a tan 9½" x 27½" rectangle as shown. Stitch the pair together on the drawn line. Fold the inner corner of the assorted print square open to form a star point; press. Trim away the excess fabric layers beneath the top triangle, leaving a ¼" seam allowance. Repeat with the remaining end of the tan rectangle to form a mirror-image point. Repeat for a total of four pieced star-point units.

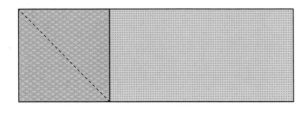

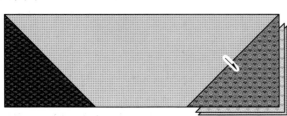

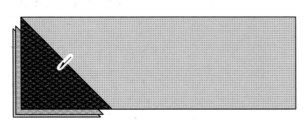

Make 4.

Preparing and Stitching the Appliqués

Refer to "Invisible Machine Appliqué" beginning on page 99 to prepare the appliqués. Pattern pieces A–D are provided on page 33.

1. Referring to "Making Bias-Tube Stems and Vines" on page 102, prepare each green 1¼"-wide bias strip.

2. Use the reserved scraps of assorted print fat quarters to prepare the following appliqués:
   + 12 flowers using pattern A. (The flower pattern isn't perfectly symmetrical; for added interest, Kim used a random mix of the flower pattern and the reversed flower pattern as she prepared her appliqués.)
   + 12 flower centers using pattern B
   + 16 berries using pattern D
   + Use the scraps from all of the green fat quarters, including those reserved from making the stems, to prepare:
     + 12 leaves using pattern C
     + 12 reversed leaves using pattern C

3. Fold each pieced star-point unit in half crosswise and use a hot iron to lightly press a center crease.

4. Select one prepared star-point unit. Dot the seam allowance of a prepared 5" stem with liquid basting glue at approximately ½" to 1" intervals, and press it onto the star-point unit, centering it over the background crease with one end flush with the bottom of the unit as shown. Position a leaf appliqué and a reversed leaf appliqué along the stem, tucking the raw edges well to the center of the stem to prevent fraying; baste in place. Referring to "Stitching Appliqués" on page 104, stitch the stem and leaves in place. Remove the

paper pattern pieces as instructed in "Removing Paper Pattern Pieces" on page 105.

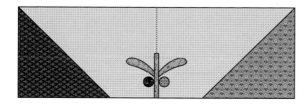

5. Working from the bottom layer to the top and using the quilt photo as a guide, lay out one flower, one flower center, one leaf, one reversed leaf, and two berries on the center stem of the star-point unit, ensuring that any layered pieces are overlapped by at least ¼". Baste and stitch the appliqués in place. Remember to remove the paper pattern pieces before adding each new layer.

6. Using the quilt photo on page 28 as a guide, use two prepared 8" stems, two flowers, two flower centers, two leaves, two reversed leaves, and two berries to lay out the remainder of the appliqué design. When you are pleased with your arrangement, work from the bottom layer to the top to baste and stitch the appliqués in place.

7. Repeat steps 4–6 for a total of four appliquéd star-point units.

Piecing the Quilt Center

1. Using the quilt photo as a guide, lay out the five Star blocks and four Hourglass blocks in three horizontal rows of three units each in alternating positions. Join the blocks in each row. Press the seam allowances open. Join the rows and press the seam allowances open.

2. Join appliquéd star-point units to the right and left sides of the quilt center. Carefully press the seam allowances toward the quilt center, taking care not to apply heat to the appliqués.

3. Join a tan 9½" square to each end of the remaining appliquéd star-point units. Press the seam allowances toward the squares. Join these pieced units to the remaining sides of the quilt center. Press the seam allowances toward the quilt center.

Piecing and Adding the Border

1. Follow steps 1–4 of "Piecing the Quilt-Center Hourglass Blocks" on page 29, and use the 180 assorted print 6¼" triangles to make 88 pieced hourglass border units measuring 5½" square, including the seam allowances. Please note that for added versatility as you assemble the units, there are four extra pieced triangles.

2. Select nine hourglass units from step 1; join the units end to end to make a pieced strip. Press the seam allowances to one side. Repeat for a total of four pieced strips.

3. Refer to the quilt assembly diagram to join the long edges of two pieced strips, reversing the direction of one strip so the seam allowances nest together. Press the seam allowances open. Repeat for a total of two pieced border strips. Join these strips to the right and left sides of the quilt center. Press the seam allowances toward the quilt center.

4. Select 13 hourglass units from step 1; join the units end to end to make a pieced strip. Press the seam allowances to one side. Repeat for a total of four pieced strips.

5. Join the long edges of two pieced strips, reversing the direction of one strip so the seam allowances nest together. Press the seam allowances open. Repeat for a total of two pieced border strips. Join these strips to the remaining sides of the quilt center. Press the seam allowances toward the quilt center. The pieced quilt top should now measure 65½" square, including the seam allowances.

Completing the Quilt

Referring to "Finishing Techniques" beginning on page 108, layer the quilt top, batting, and backing.

Quilt the layers. The featured quilt was machine quilted with feathered wreaths stitched onto each quilt center patchwork and setting block, and the open areas of the block corners were quilted with curved concentric squares. The appliqués were outlined to emphasize their shapes, and the open tan background areas behind the appliqués were stitched with a McTavish design (free-form shapes that echo inward); a 1" crosshatch was stitched onto each star point. The border was quilted with a curved feathered vine. Join the seven black 2½" x 42" strips into one length and use it to bind the quilt.

Quilt assembly

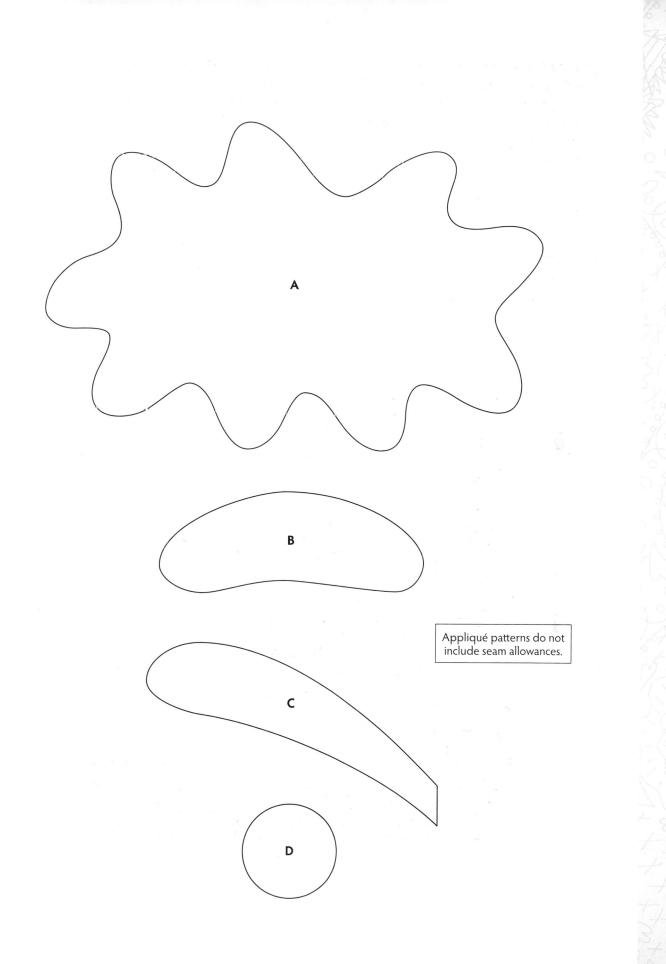

A

B

Appliqué patterns do not
include seam allowances.

C

D

Country Haven

*C*reate a haven meant for snuggling with this not-quite-traditional Log Cabin–style quilt. Strips of colorful prints and soothing neutrals combine with gently blooming daisies on the vine to bring a touch of easy, unassuming elegance to this easily stitched lap quilt.

Materials

21 fat quarters (18" x 22") of assorted prints for blocks, appliqués, and binding
½ yard *each* of 4 neutral prints for blocks
1¼ yards of black print for blocks and vines
2 yards of medium-green print for blocks and border
4⅔ yards of fabric for backing
84" x 84" square of batting
Bias bar to fit your vines
Appliqué supplies (see page 99)

Cutting

Cut all strips across the width of the fabric in the order given unless otherwise noted. For greater ease in preparation, cutting instructions are provided separately for the appliqués.

From the *lengthwise grain* of the medium-green print, cut:
4 strips, 8½" x 60½"
Reserve the remainder of the medium-green print for the blocks.

From the 21 assorted print fat quarters and the remainder of the medium-green print, cut a *combined total* of:
104 rectangles, 1½" x 8½"
72 rectangles, 1½" x 6½"
72 rectangles, 1½" x 4½"
72 rectangles, 1½" x 2½"
Enough 2½"-wide random-length strips to make a 314" length of binding when pieced together end to end using straight, not diagonal, seams
Reserve the scraps for the appliqués.

From the neutral prints, cut a *combined total* of:
36 rectangles, 2½" x 8½"
36 rectangles, 2½" x 6½"
36 rectangles, 2½" x 4½"
36 squares, 2½" x 2½"

From the black print, cut:
12 strips, 2½" x 42"; crosscut into 180 squares, 2½" x 2½"
Enough 1¼"-wide *bias* strips to make 4 lengths measuring 60" each when pieced together end to end using straight, not diagonal, seams

Piecing the Blocks

Sew all pieces with right sides together using a ¼" seam allowance unless otherwise noted.

1. Select two assorted print 1½" x 8½" rectangles. Join the pair along the long edges. Press the seam allowances to one side. Repeat for a total of 36 pieced 8½" units. Set aside the remainder of the 1½" x 8½" rectangles for the border pieced corner squares.

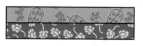

Make 36.

"Country Haven"

FINISHED QUILT SIZE: 76½" x 76½"

FINISHED BLOCK SIZE: 10" x 10"

Designed, pieced, and machine appliquéd by Kim Diehl.
Machine quilted by the staff at The Gathering Place in Rupert, Idaho.

2. Repeat step 1 to make a total of 36 pieced rectangle units *each* in 6½", 4½", and 2½" lengths.

3. Lay out one pieced rectangle unit of each length, five black 2½" squares, one neutral print rectangle in each length, and one neutral print 2½" square in five horizontal rows as shown. Join the pieces in each row. Press the seam allowances toward the black square. Join the rows. Press the seam allowances toward the 8½" pieced rectangle unit. Repeat for a total of 36 blocks measuring 10½" square, including the seam allowances.

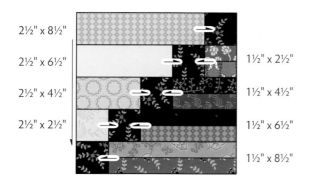

2½" x 8½"

2½" x 6½"   1½" x 2½"

2½" x 4½"   1½" x 4½"

2½" x 2½"   1½" x 6½"

1½" x 8½"

Make 36.

Piecing the Quilt Center

Lay out the blocks in six horizontal rows of six blocks each, turning every other block. Join the blocks in each row. Press the seam allowances of each row toward the blocks with the vertical strips. Join the rows. Press the seam allowances open.

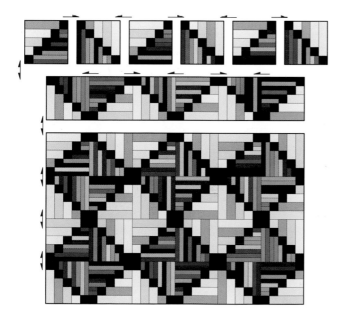

Appliquéing and Adding the Border

Refer to page 39 for appliqué patterns A and B, and to "Invisible Machine Appliqué" on page 99 for pattern piece preparation and stitching.

1. Use the reserved assorted print scraps to prepare the following appliqués:
   + 48 leaves using pattern A
   + 20 flower petals using pattern A
   + 24 berries using pattern B
   + 4 flower centers using pattern B

2. Join the black bias strips end to end using straight, not diagonal, seams to make four lengths, 60" each. Referring to "Making Bias-Tube Stems and Vines" on page 102, prepare the vines.

Perfectly Prepared Appliqué Points

Occasionally, depending upon the shape of your appliqué and the fabric used to prepare it, the seam allowance at a point will need a little bit of extra coaxing to help it stay in place. After I've prepared and pressed any given point, if the seam allowance is lifting a bit and not firmly anchored to the back of the appliqué, I'll dip the tip of my awl into a fabric glue stick and use it to add an extra little dollop where needed. Give the re-glued area a quick press with a hot iron, and the point will be sharp and crisp, with the seam allowance anchored perfectly in place.

3. Fold a green 8½" x 60½" strip in half lengthwise, right sides together, and use a hot, dry iron to press a center crease. Dot the seam of a prepared black stem with liquid basting glue at approximately ½" to 1" intervals. Beginning at the left-hand side of the strip, with the vine and border edges flush, press the prepared vine onto the cloth to make a serpentine shape along the center crease. Trim away any excess vine length to achieve the look you desire.

4. Using the quilt photo on page 36 as a guide, lay out 12 prepared leaf appliqués and six prepared berry appliqués along the vine. When you are pleased with your design, baste the appliqués in place, referring to "Basting Appliqués" on page 103. Stitch the vines, leaves, and berries in place; remove the paper pattern pieces as instructed in "Removing Paper Pattern Pieces" on page 105. Work from the bottom layer to the top to position, baste, and stitch five flower petal appliqués and one flower center, ensuring that any layered pieces are overlapped by at least ¼".

5. Repeat steps 3 and 4 to appliqué a total of four border strips.

6. Join eight assorted print 1½" x 8½" rectangles along the long edges. Press the seam allowances in one direction. Repeat for a total of four pieced corner squares.

Make 4.

7. Referring to the quilt photo, join appliquéd border strips to the right and left sides of the quilt center. Carefully press the seam allowances toward the border. Join a pieced corner square to each end of the remaining appliquéd border strips. Press the seam allowances toward the appliquéd border strips. Join these pieced border strips to the remaining sides of the quilt center. Press the seam allowances toward the border. The pieced and appliquéd quilt top should now measure 76½" square, including the seam allowances.

Completing the Quilt

Referring to "Finishing Techniques" on page 108 for any details needed, layer the quilt top, batting, and backing. Quilt the layers. The featured quilt was machine quilted with small-scale feathered wreaths in the center of the neutral print areas, the black squares were quilted with Xs, and a tiny stippled design was used as filler on the remaining areas of the quilt center. The appliqués were outlined and details such as veining were added to the leaves, berries, and flower centers, and the border was echo quilted. Join the random lengths of assorted print 2½"-wide strips to make a 314" strip and use it to bind the quilt.

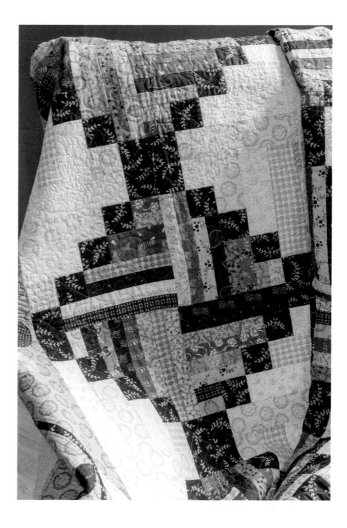

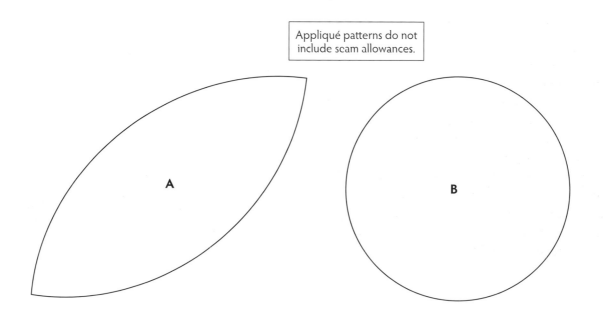

Appliqué patterns do not include seam allowances.

A

B

Penny Candy

*S*crappy Nine Patch blocks and horizontal stripes of scarlet work hand in hand to create this humble yet appealing bed quilt reminiscent of simpler, gentler times.

Materials

3¾ yards of neutral print for patchwork and setting squares

2⅞ yards of dark print or stripe for sashing strips and binding

16 fat eighths (9" x 22") of assorted prints for patchwork

5 yards of fabric for backing

78" x 90" rectangle of batting

Cutting

Cut all strips across the width of the fabric in the order given unless otherwise noted.

From *each* of the 16 assorted print fat eighths, cut:

3 strips, 2½" x 22" (combined total of 48). Keep the strips organized by print.

From the neutral print, cut:

24 strips, 2½" x 42"; crosscut *each* strip into 2 strips, 2½" x 21" (48 total)

10 strips, 6½" x 42"; crosscut into 60 squares, 6½" x 6½"

From the *lengthwise grain* of the dark print or stripe, cut:

6 strips, 4½" x 72½"

From the remainder of the dark print or stripe, cut:

8 binding strips, 2½" x 42"

Piecing the Nine Patch Blocks

Sew all pieces with right sides together using a ¼" seam allowance unless otherwise noted.

1. Select three matching assorted print 2½" x 22" strips and three neutral print 2½" x 21" strips.

2. Join a matching print strip to each long side of a neutral print strip to make strip set A. Press the seam allowances toward the matching print strips. Crosscut the strip set into eight segments, 2½" wide.

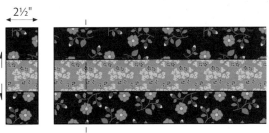

Strip set A.
Make 1. Cut 8 segments.

3. Join a neutral print strip to each long side of the remaining assorted print strip to make strip set B. Press the seam allowances toward the assorted print strip. Crosscut the strip set into four segments, 2½" wide.

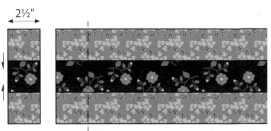

Strip set B.
Make 1. Cut 4 segments.

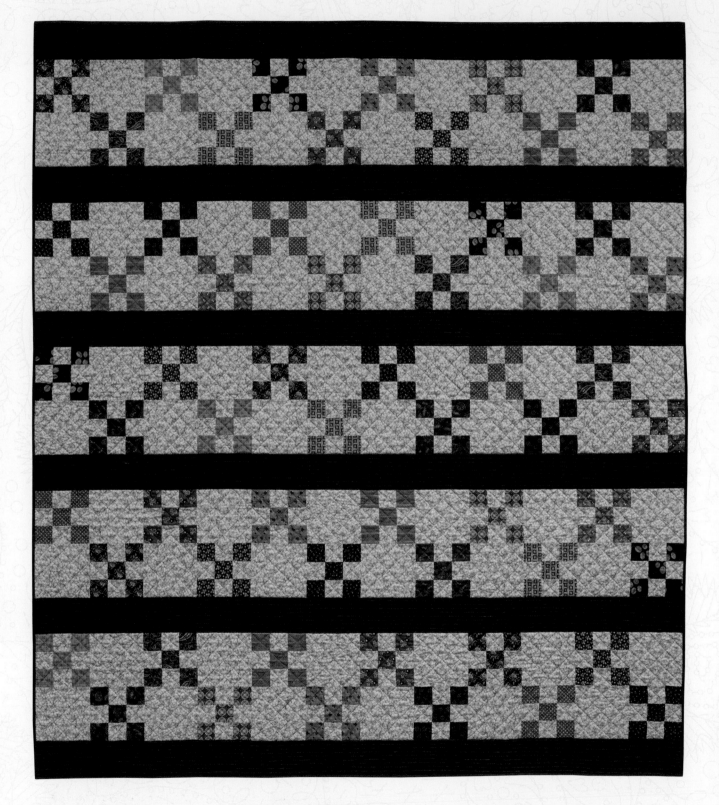

"Penny Candy"

FINISHED QUILT SIZE: 72½" x 84½"

FINISHED BLOCK SIZE: 6" x 6"

Designed by Kim Diehl. Pieced by Deb Behrend. Machine quilted by Deborah Poole.

4. Lay out two A segments from step 2 and one B segment from step 3 as shown. Join the rows. Press the seam allowances away from the middle row. Repeat for a total of four pieced Nine Patch blocks measuring 6½" square, including the seam allowances.

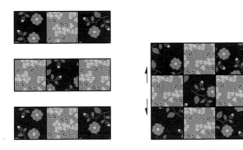

Make 4.

5. Repeat steps 1–4 to make a total of 64 Nine Patch blocks.

Piecing the Block Rows

1. Beginning with a Nine Patch block, lay out six assorted print Nine Patch blocks and six neutral print 6½" squares in alternating positions. Join the pieces. Press the seam allowances toward the neutral print squares. Repeat for a total of 10 pieced strips measuring 6½" x 72½", including the seam allowances. Please note that there will be four unused Nine Patch blocks after the strips have been pieced; these have been included to give you versatility as the strips are assembled.

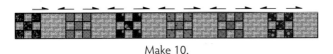

Make 10.

2. Select two pieced strips from step 1. Using the quilt photo on page 42 as a guide, reverse the direction of one pieced strip to stagger the placement of the Nine Patch blocks. Join the strips along the long edges. Press the seam allowances open. Repeat for a total of five pieced block rows measuring 12½" x 72½", including the seam allowances.

Piecing the Quilt Top

Referring to the quilt photo, lay out the six dark print or stripe 4½" x 72½" strips and five pieced block rows in alternating positions. Join the rows. Press the seam allowances toward the dark strips. The pieced quilt top should now measure 72½" x 84½", including the seam allowances.

Completing the Quilt

Referring to "Finishing Techniques" on page 108 for any details needed, layer the quilt top, batting, and backing. Quilt the layers. The featured quilt was machine quilted with a crosshatch stitched through the Nine Patch blocks and setting squares, and the sashing strips were stitched with gently curved asymmetrical serpentine feathered vines. Join the eight dark print or stripe 2½" x 42" wide strips into one length and use it to bind the quilt.

Homestead Harvest

*S*ubtle cream and beige strips are the perfect backdrop for bold, richly colored patchwork, and curving vines of blossoming wool pomegranates and berries are the icing on the quilt cake. You'll find this wall quilt easy to stitch, and even easier to live with.

Materials

12 fat quarters (18" x 22") of assorted tan prints for block and border patchwork

32 squares, 5½" x 5½", of assorted medium and dark prints for block and border patchwork

1 fat quarter of green print for vines

5 squares, 4" x 4", of assorted-color wools for penny appliqués

5 squares, 3" x 3", of assorted-color wools for penny appliqués

5 squares, 1½" x 1½", of assorted-color wools for penny appliqués

4 rectangles, 4" x 5", of assorted medium-cranberry wools for pomegranate and berry appliqués

5 rectangles, 3" x 8", of assorted dark-cranberry wools for berry appliqués

6 rectangles, 5" x 8", of assorted green wools for leaf appliqués

4 squares, 2½" x 2½", of assorted orange wools for pomegranate center appliqués

½ yard of black print for binding

2⅞ yards of fabric for backing*

45" x 45" square of batting

Bias bar to fit your vines

Approximately ½ yard of HeatnBond Lite iron-on adhesive

Size 5 embroidery needle

#12 perle cotton for stitching the wool appliqués and hand quilting (I used Valdani's #12 variegated perle cotton in H212 Faded Brown and P3 Aged White Medium)

Appliqué supplies (see page 99)

If you don't prewash your fabric and it has a selvage-to-selvage measurement of at least 44", you can reduce this amount to 1¼ yards.

Cutting

Cut all pieces across the width of the fabric in the order given unless otherwise noted. For greater ease in preparation, cutting instructions for the wool appliqués are provided separately.

From *each* of the 12 tan print fat quarters, cut:
5 strips, 1½" x 22" (combined total of 60)

From the remainder of the tan fat quarters (and using a variety of prints for each size of piece needed), cut a *combined total* of:
4 rectangles, 1½" x 10½"
8 rectangles, 1½" x 9½"
8 rectangles, 1½" x 8½"
8 rectangles, 1½" x 7½"
8 rectangles, 1½" x 6½"
12 rectangles, 1½" x 5½"
16 rectangles, 1½" x 4½"
16 rectangles, 1½" x 3½"
16 rectangles, 1½" x 2½"
16 squares, 1½" x 1½"

From the *bias* of the green print fat quarter, cut:
4 strips, 1¼" x 16"
4 strips, 1¼" x 14"

From the black print, cut:
5 binding strips, 2½" x 42"

"Homestead Harvest"

FINISHED QUILT SIZE: 40½" x 40½"

Designed, pieced, machine and hand appliquéd, and hand quilted by Kim Diehl.

Piecing the Background Units

Sew all pieces with right sides together using a ¼" seam allowance unless otherwise noted.

1. Select 10 strips from assorted tan prints. Join the strips along the long edges to make strip set A. Press the seam allowances in one direction. Repeat for a total of two A strip sets. Crosscut the strip sets into four segments, 10½" wide.

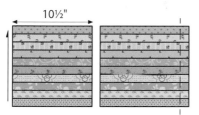

Strip set A.
Make 2. Cut 4 segments.

PIN POINT

Accurately Pieced Strips

I find that strip sets, especially those pieced from many strips, can often finish slightly smaller than the mathematically correct size because of the cloth that is sometimes lost to the folds when numerous seam allowances are pressed. To help ensure my strip sets finish at the correct size, I routinely use a seam allowance that's a thread or two less than ¼" as I begin my project, and then I measure the width of my first completed strip set for accuracy. If the measurement of my pieced strip set is off, I make the necessary adjustments to my seam allowance before continuing. I've discovered that it's worth taking an extra moment to check my accuracy when I'm in the early stages of a project, rather than having to "unsew" my patchwork later when there are units that don't fit together quite right.

2. Select five strips from assorted tan prints. Join the strips to make strip set B. Press the seam allowances in one direction. Repeat for a total of eight B strip sets. Crosscut the strip sets into 20 segments, 5½" wide, and four segments, 10½" wide.

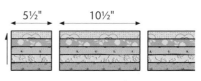

Strip set B. Make 8.
Cut 20 segments, 5½" wide, and 4 segments, 10½" wide.

3. Join two tan 1½" squares. Press the seam allowances to one side. Join a tan 1½" x 2½" rectangle to the joined squares. Press the seam allowances toward the rectangle. Join a second tan 1½" x 2½" rectangle to the adjacent side of the first rectangle. Press the seam allowances toward the newly added rectangle. Continue adding progressively larger rectangles to the pieced unit, always joining them to the side with one seam, and pressing the seam allowances toward the newly added rectangle. Repeat for a total of four pieced quilt-center corner squares measuring 10½" x 10½", including the seam allowances.

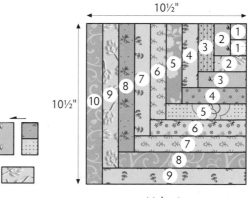

Make 4.

4. Repeat step 3 to make a total of four pieced border corner squares measuring 5½" x 5½", including the seam allowances.

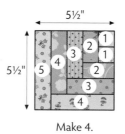

Make 4.

Piecing the Quilt Center

1. Lay out four strip set B segments measuring 5½" square in two horizontal rows of two units each to form the star center. Join the pieces in each row. Press the seam allowances away from the edge with the multiple seams. Join the rows. Press the seam allowances open.

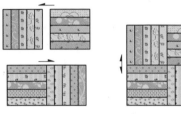

2. Use a pencil and an acrylic ruler to draw a diagonal line from corner to corner on the wrong side of each assorted print 5½" square.

3. Layer a prepared assorted print 5½" square onto one corner of a 10½" strip set A segment as shown. Stitch the pair together on the drawn line. Press the resulting triangle open, aligning the corner with the bottom layers to keep it square. Trim away the excess layers underneath the top triangle, leaving a ¼" seam allowance. Repeat to layer, press, and trim an additional prepared assorted print square on the opposite adjacent corner as shown. Repeat for a total of four pieced star-point units. Reserve the remaining prepared assorted print 5½" squares for later use.

Make 4.

4. Lay out the star-center square, four pieced star-point units, and four 10½" pieced corner squares in three horizontal rows as shown. Join the pieces in each row. Press the seam allowances away from the star points. Join the rows. Press the

seam allowances away from the middle row. The pieced quilt center should now measure 30½" square, including the seam allowances.

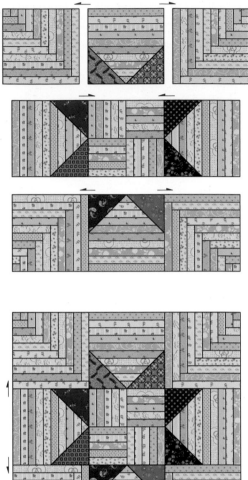

Preparing the Wool Appliqués

Refer to page 51 for appliqué pattern pieces A–F, and to "Preparing Wool Appliqués" on page 106 for appliqué preparation.

Using the quilt photo on page 46 as a guide, prepare the following appliqués from the assorted wool squares and rectangles:

+ 5 pennies from assorted colors using pattern A
+ 5 pennies from assorted colors using pattern B
+ 5 pennies from assorted colors using pattern C
+ 4 pomegranates from assorted medium cranberries using pattern D
+ 44 berries from assorted dark cranberries and scraps of medium cranberries using pattern C
+ 32 leaves from assorted greens using pattern E
+ 4 pomegranate centers from assorted oranges using pattern E
+ 4 oak leaves and 4 reversed oak leaves from assorted greens using pattern F

Stitching the Penny and Pomegranate Units

1. Using the quilt photo as a guide and referring to "Wool Appliqué" beginning on page 106, layer, glue baste, heat set, and stitch five stacked A, B, and C wool penny units.

2. Stitch an orange E center appliqué onto each pomegranate, for a total of four stitched pomegranate units.

Appliquéing the Quilt Center

1. Referring to "Making Bias-Tube Stems and Vines" on page 102, prepare each 1¼"-wide green bias strip.

2. Fold the quilt top in half diagonally and use a hot, dry iron to lightly press a crease from corner to corner. Refold and press a second diagonal crease to form an X.

3. To stabilize the quilt top as you stitch your wool, use your sewing machine to stay stitch each corner block of the quilt top about ⅛" in from the raw edges.

4. Using the quilt photo as a guide, and the background strips for easy and consistent placement, position a stitched penny unit onto each corner of the quilt top; pin in place. Position a stitched penny unit in the center square; pin in place.

5. Dot the seam allowance of a prepared 16" stem with liquid basting glue at approximately ½" to 1" intervals. Referring to the quilt photo, position the vine onto the quilt top, letting it curve slightly along the pressed crease and tucking the raw ends under the center and corner penny stacks approximately ¼"; trim away any excess stem length. Repeat with the remaining corners. Glue baste and add a 14" vine to each of the 16" vines, ensuring each raw edge is tucked

well under the original stem to prevent fraying. Remove the penny units. Referring to "Stitching Appliqués" on page 104, stitch the stems in place.

6. Reposition and glue baste the penny units. Referring to "Stitching Wool Appliqués" on page 107, stitch the penny units to the quilt top. Next, position, baste, and stitch the pomegranate units to the quilt top. Last, position, baste, and stitch the leaves, reversed leaves, and berries, using the quilt photo as a guide.

Piecing and Adding the Border

1. With right sides together, layer a reserved assorted print 5½" square onto a 5½" strip set B segment as shown. Stitch the pair together on the drawn line. Press and trim as previously instructed. Repeat for a total of eight left-facing point units and eight right-facing point units.

Make 8.　　Make 8.

2. Using two prepared assorted print 5½" squares and one 10½" strip set B segment, repeat step 3 of "Piecing the Quilt Center" to make a pieced star-point unit. Repeat for a total of four units.

Make 4.

3. Referring to the quilt photo, lay out one pieced star-point unit, two right-facing point units, and two left-facing point units to make a border strip. Join the units. Press the seam allowances away from the points. Repeat for a total of four pieced border strips.

4. Join pieced border strips to the right and left sides of the quilt center. Press the seam allowances toward the quilt center. Using the quilt photo as a guide, join a pieced border corner square to each end of the remaining border rows. Press the seam allowances away from the points. Join these rows to the remaining sides of the quilt center. The pieced quilt top should now measure 40½" square, including the seam allowances.

Completing the Quilt

Referring to "Finishing Techniques" on page 108 for any details needed, layer the quilt top, batting, and backing. Quilt the layers. The featured quilt was hand quilted using the big-stitch method (see page 109) and the Faded Brown perle cotton for the star points and appliqués, and the Aged White perle cotton on the tan background areas. The patchwork was stitched in the ditch (along the seam lines), the appliqués were outlined to emphasize their shape, and the star points were quilted with straight lines that repeated at ½" intervals. Join the five black 2½" x 42" strips into one length and use it to bind the quilt.

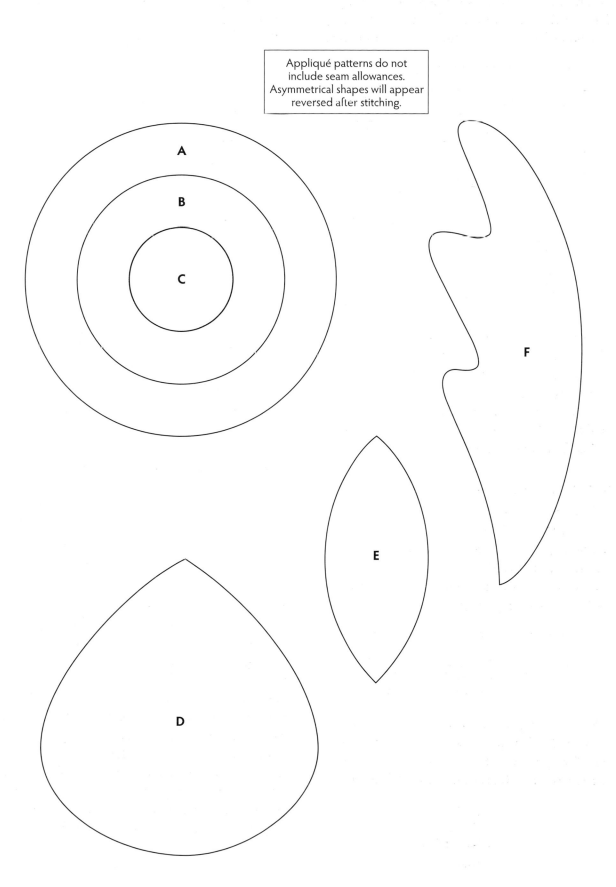

Appliqué patterns do not
include seam allowances.
Asymmetrical shapes will appear
reversed after stitching.

A

B

C

F

E

D

Lunch Box Social

*F*un-to-stitch patchwork blocks, a myriad of prints, and striped sashing-strip accents come together seamlessly in this cheerful little table topper. Lay it on a table, add a simple centerpiece, and enjoy a dollop of instant warmth and charm.

Materials
18 chubby sixteenths (9" x 11") of assorted prints for blocks and nine-patch units

⅞ yard of tan print for blocks

⅔ yard of small-scale medium-hued stripe or print for blocks and sashing strips

½ yard of dark-blue print (or a complementary color of your choosing) for nine-patch unit center squares and binding

½ yard of large-scale stripe or print in a complementary color for border

2⅞ yards of fabric for backing*

45" x 45" square of batting

If you don't prewash your fabric and it has a selvage-to-selvage measurement of at least 44", you can reduce this amount to 1¼ yards.

Cutting
Cut all strips across the width of the fabric in the order given unless otherwise noted.

From the tan print, cut:
4 strips, 1½" x 42"; crosscut 2 of the strips into 34 squares, 1½" x 1½"

4 strips, 2⅜" x 42"; crosscut into 54 squares, 2⅜" x 2⅜". Cut each square in half diagonally *once* to yield 108 triangles.

4 strips, 2" x 42"; crosscut into 36 rectangles, 2" x 3½"

From the dark-blue print, cut:
1 strip, 1½" x 42"

5 binding strips, 2½" x 42"

From *each* of the 18 assorted print chubby sixteenths, cut:
1 strip, 3½" x 11"; crosscut into:
   2 squares, 3½" x 3½" (combined total of 36)
   4 squares, 1½" x 1½" (combined total of 72)
1 strip, 2⅜" x 11"; crosscut into 3 squares, 2⅜" x 2⅜". Cut each square in half diagonally *once* to yield 6 triangles (combined total of 108).

Keep the pieces organized by print.

From the small-scale medium-hued stripe or print, cut:
5 strips, 2" x 42"; crosscut into:
   18 rectangles, 2" x 3½"
   18 rectangles, 2" x 6½"
3 strips, 3½" x 42"; crosscut into 12 rectangles, 3½" x 9½"

From the large-scale stripe or print, cut:
4 strips, 3½" x 33½"

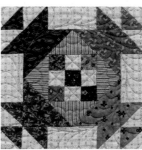

"Lunch Box Social"

FINISHED QUILT SIZE: 39½" x 39½"

FINISHED BLOCK SIZE: 9" x 9"

Designed by Kim Diehl. Pieced by Barbara Walsh and Kim Diehl. Machine quilted by Deborah Poole.

Piecing the Nine-Patch Units

Sew all pieces with right sides together using a ¼" seam allowance unless otherwise noted.

1. Join a tan 1½" x 42" strip to each long side of the dark-blue 1½" x 42" strip to make a strip set. Press the seam allowances toward the dark-blue strip. Crosscut the strip set into 17 segments, 1½" wide.

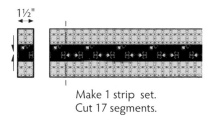

Make 1 strip set.
Cut 17 segments.

2. Join assorted print 1½" squares to opposite sides of a tan 1½" square. Press the seam allowances toward the assorted print squares. Repeat for a total of 34 pieced units measuring 1½" x 3½", including the seam allowances. Please note that you'll have four unused assorted print squares; these have been included for added versatility as you piece your nine-patch units.

Make 34.

3. Lay out two pieced units from step 2 and one strip-set unit from step 1 into three horizontal rows as shown. Join the rows. Press the seam allowances away from the middle row. Repeat for a total of 17 pieced nine-patch units measuring 3½" square, including the seam allowances.

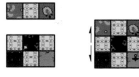

Make 17.

Piecing the Half-Square-Triangle Units

Stitch each assorted print triangle to a tan triangle along the long diagonal edges. Press the seam allowances toward the assorted print triangle. Trim away the dog-ear points. Repeat for a total of 108 pieced half-square-triangle units measuring 2" x 2", including the seam allowances. For greater ease in piecing the blocks, keep these units organized by print.

Make 108.

Piecing the Blocks

1. Join small-scale stripe 2" x 3½" rectangles to the right and left sides of a pieced nine-patch unit. Press the seam allowances away from the nine-patch unit. Join a small-scale stripe 2" x 6½" rectangle to the remaining sides of the nine-patch unit. Press the seam allowances away from the nine-patch unit. Repeat for a total of nine pieced center units. Reserve the remaining nine-patch units for later use.

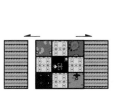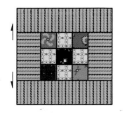

Make 9.

2. Use a pencil and an acrylic ruler to draw a diagonal line from corner to corner on the wrong side of each assorted print 3½" square.

3. Layer prepared assorted print squares on two opposite corners of a pieced center unit. Stitch, press, and trim as instructed in "Pressing Triangle Units" on page 98. In the same manner, stitch a prepared assorted print 3½" square onto the remaining corners of the center unit. Repeat for a total of nine block center units measuring 6½" square, including the seam allowances.

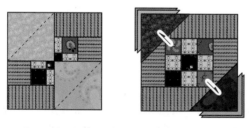

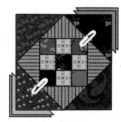

Make 9.

4. Lay out a center unit from step 3, 12 half-square-triangle units (three each of the four colors that match the pieced center unit corners), and four tan 2" x 3½" rectangles as shown. Join the half-square-triangles and tan rectangles on each side of the center unit. Press the seam allowances toward the rectangles. Join these units to the sides of the center unit to make the middle row. Press the seam allowances away from the center unit. Join the pieces in the top and bottom rows. Press the seam allowances toward the rectangles. Join the rows. Press the seam allowances away from the middle row. Repeat for a total of nine pieced blocks measuring 9½" square, including the seam allowances.

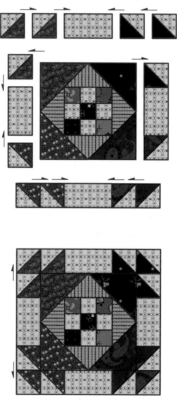

Make 9.

Piecing the Quilt Top

1. Lay out three pieced blocks and two small-scale stripe 3½" x 9½" rectangles in alternating positions. Join the pieces. Press the seam allowances toward the rectangles. Repeat for a total of three block rows measuring 9½" x 33½", including the seam allowances.

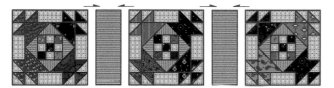

Make 3.

2. Lay out three small-scale stripe 3½" x 9½" rectangles and two reserved nine-patch units in alternating positions. Join the pieces. Press the seam allowances toward the rectangles. Repeat for a total of two pieced sashing rows measuring 3½" x 33½", including the seam allowances.

Make 2.

3. Using the quilt photo on page 54 as a guide, alternately lay out the pieced block rows and the pieced sashing rows to form the quilt center. Join the rows. Press the seam allowances toward the sashing rows.

4. Join large-scale stripe 3½" x 33½" strips to the right and left sides of the quilt center. Press the seam allowances toward the large-scale stripe strips.

5. Join a reserved nine-patch unit to each end of the remaining two large-scale stripe strips. Press the seam allowances away from the nine-patch units. Join these pieced strips to the remaining sides of the quilt center. Press the seam allowances toward the newly added pieced strips. The pieced quilt top should now measure 39½" square, including the seam allowances.

Completing the Quilt

Referring to "Finishing Techniques" on page 108 for any details needed, layer the quilt top, batting, and backing. Quilt the layers. The featured quilt was machine quilted with square feathered wreaths in each block and cross hatching through all of the nine-patch centers, including those in the sashing intersections and border corner blocks. The sashing and border were quilted in straight lines that follow the stripes, repeated at regular intervals to emphasize the patterns. Join the five dark-blue 2½" x 42" strips into one length and use it to bind the quilt.

Patty-Cakes Pincushion

A perfect gift for a friend (or even a treat for yourself), this little pincushion is incredibly quick to fashion, and a sweet and simple way to repurpose a vintage zinc jar lid. Gather your scraps, and start stitching!

FINISHED PINCUSHION: Approximately 3¼" x 3"
Designed and made by Kim Diehl.

Materials

16 assorted print 5" charm squares
Freezer paper
Vintage zinc jar lid, approximately 3" in diameter
#8 or #12 perle cotton
Size 5 embroidery needle
Crushed walnut shells for filler
Scotch tape
Two-hole button of your choice
Hot-glue gun and glue stick

Cutting and Preparing the Pincushion Wedges

Refer to page 61 for the large and small pincushion wedge patterns.

1. Lay a piece of freezer paper, dull side up, over the large wedge pattern. Use a pencil and an acrylic ruler to trace the straight lines onto the freezer paper; finish the shape by tracing the curved line where it meets the straight edges. Stack seven additional pieces of freezer paper, all with the dull sides up, under the top piece with the traced shape. Anchor the layers with a straight pin, and use an acrylic ruler and a rotary cutter to cut along the straight edges of the traced pattern; use scissors to cut along the curved edge. Repeat with the small wedge pattern to make eight freezer-paper pattern pieces.

2. Use a hot, dry iron to adhere each large and small freezer-paper wedge onto the wrong side of an assorted print charm square. Use an acrylic ruler and a rotary cutter to cut out the fabric wedges, adding a ¼" seam allowance to each straight side; cut the curved edges exactly on the drawn lines, without adding a seam allowance. Leave the paper pattern pieces in place.

Stitching the Pincushion Units

Stitch all pieces with right sides together using a ¼" seam allowance. Because the pincushion will be filled with crushed walnut shells, Kim recommends reducing your stitch length slightly to achieve sewn seams that will remain secure and keep the filler firmly in place.

1. Select two large prepared wedge pieces. Pin the wedges together along one straight side, lining up the paper pattern pieces exactly. Repeat with the remaining large wedges to make four pinned pairs.

2. Beginning at the points and starting and ending with a couple of backstitches, stitch each pair together exactly next to the pattern edges. Do not press the seam allowances or remove the pattern pieces at this time. Next, in the same manner, join two stitched pairs. Repeat to make two pieced units of four wedges each. Press the seam allowances of the outer two seams away from the center of the pieced unit. Press the center seam allowances open.

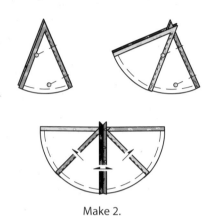

Make 2.

3. Line up the two stitched and pressed halves and pin them together along the straight edges. Stitch the halves together from edge to edge exactly along the pattern pieces. Peel away the paper pattern pieces, trim away the dog-ear points at the intersections of the seams, and press the center seam allowances open.

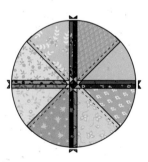

4. Repeat steps 1–3 using the small wedge pieces.

Preparing and Filling the Pincushion Tiers

1. From the right side of the large pieced circle, use a double strand of perle cotton and an embroidery needle to sew a running stitch ⅛" from the outer edge of the unit; leave a thread tail 3" to 4" long where you begin and end the stitches. (Taking stitches approximately ¼" long will enable the gathers to be pulled tightly together and leave a smaller center opening.)

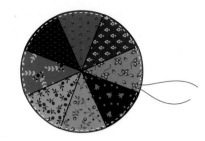

2. Pull on the thread tails to gather the stitches until the opening is approximately 1" in diameter. Fill the unit with crushed walnut shells. Pull the stitches taut to make a very small opening. Knot the thread tails securely and place a square of Scotch tape over the opening to prevent any shells from escaping.

3. Repeat steps 1 and 2 with the small pieced circle.

Assembling the Pincushion

1. Heat up the hot-glue gun.

2. With the filled pieced circles both positioned gathered side up, place the large pieced circle on top of the small pieced circle, aligning the seams. Use a long double strand of perle cotton and an embroidery needle to place a long stitch through the gathered fabric at the center of the layered tiers, beginning with the small pieced circle and leaving a long thread tail. After the needle exits the large pieced circle through the gathered edge, bring the needle back up through the tiers, again stitching through the gathered fabric across from the first stitch, and bringing it out at the top center of the small tier. Thread the perle cotton through the holes of the button, pull the perle cotton taught to bring the tiers together, and tie a secure double (or even triple!) knot at the button to anchor it in place. Clip the thread, leaving a bit of a decorative tail.

3. Carefully apply a large blob of hot glue to the inside center of the zinc lid and nestle the gathered side of the large tier into it, pressing down on the pincushion from the top for several

minutes while the glue cools and anchors the pincushion in place. Carefully lift the edge of the top tier and place several dots of hot glue between the fabric layers (toward the center of the pincushion so they'll be hidden), spacing the glue at even intervals. Press the top tier down for a moment or two while the glue cools to set the layers together.

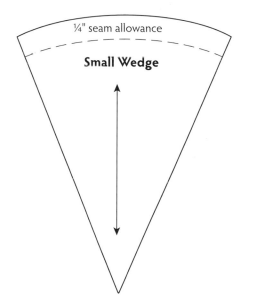

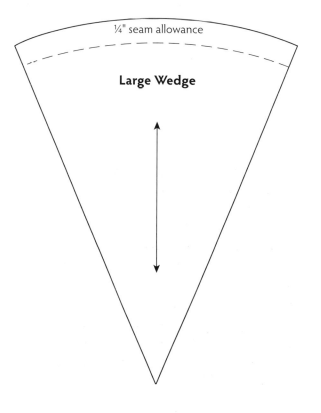

PIN POINT

Turning Small Orphan Blocks into Pincushions

It's easy to recycle leftover orphan blocks and turn them into adorable little pincushions. Simply cut a piece of backing cloth approximately ½" larger than your block, layer the pieces right sides together, and stitch along the raw block edges using a ¼" seam allowance, leaving an opening approximately 2" wide for filling the pincushion. Press each corner of the stitched unit flat from the side and sew a line through the block and backing seams to miter the corner, just a little bit inside of the points (depending upon the size of your block, usually about ½" to 1" is perfect); the further in from the point you stitch this seam, the fuller your pincushion will be. Trim away the points at each corner seam, leaving a ¼" seam allowance. Turn the pincushion right side out, fill with crushed walnut shells or batting, and sew the opening closed using tiny stitches and matching thread. For an added touch, use a double strand of perle cotton to stitch a button through the center of the pincushion, knot it, and leave a decorative thread tail. These little pincushions are fast and fun to stitch, and they make great gifts for quilting friends.

Apple Brown Betty

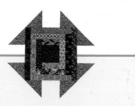

*T*riangles of warm golden brown, accents of apple red, and quick-to-stitch blocks make this the perfect project for some instant patchwork gratification. Snuggle into your finished quilt with a good book and a mug of cocoa, and while away the day.

Materials

33 fat eighths (9" x 22") of assorted prints for blocks
1 yard of chocolate-brown print for blocks, sashing squares, and binding
1 yard of dark-tan print for blocks
⅔ yard of light-tan print for sashing strips
⅝ yard of red print for blocks and border
⅝ yard of light-brown print for blocks
4 yards of fabric for backing
73" x 73" square of batting

Cutting

Cut all pieces across the width of the fabric in the order given unless otherwise noted.

From the red print, cut:
3 strips, 3½" x 42"; crosscut into 33 squares, 3½" x 3½"
3 strips, 2½" x 42"; crosscut into 36 squares, 2½" x 2½"

From *each* of the 33 assorted print fat eighths, refer to the cutting diagram below to cut:
2 A rectangles, 1½" x 3½" (combined total of 66)
4 B rectangles, 1½" x 5½" (combined total of 132)
4 C rectangles, 1½" x 7½" (combined total of 132)
2 D rectangles, 1½" x 9½" (combined total of 66)

D			D		
C		C		A	
C		C		A	
B		B		B	
B					

From the scraps of the assorted print fat eighths, cut:
8 rectangles, 1½" x 9½"
Cut additional A, B, C, and D rectangles (sizes given above) from the remainder of the scraps for added versatility during the piecing process.

From the light-brown print, cut:
4 strips, 3⅞" x 42"; crosscut into 36 squares, 3⅞" x 3⅞". Cut each square in half diagonally *once* to yield 72 triangles.

From the dark-tan print, cut:
4 strips, 3⅞" x 42"; crosscut into 36 squares, 3⅞" x 3⅞". Cut each square in half diagonally *once* to yield 72 triangles.
4 strips, 3½" x 42"; crosscut into 36 squares, 3½" x 3½"

From the chocolate-brown print, cut:
7 strips, 1½" x 42"; crosscut into:
    36 rectangles, 1½" x 2½"
    36 rectangles, 1½" x 3½"
    16 squares, 1½" x 1½"
7 binding strips, 2½" x 42"

From the light-tan print, cut:
14 strips, 1½" x 42"; crosscut into:
    24 strips, 1½" x 15½"
    8 strips, 1½" x 9½"

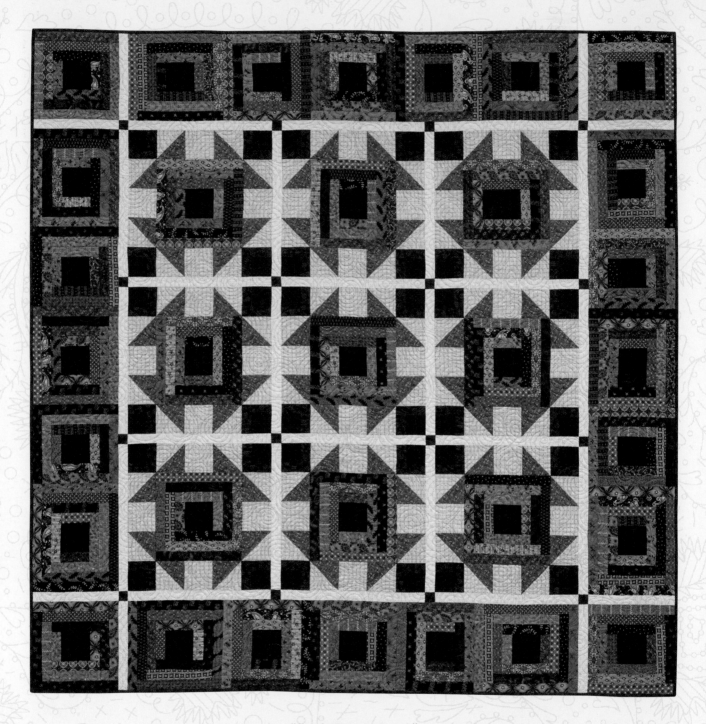

"Apple Brown Betty"
FINISHED QUILT SIZE: 67½" x 67½"
FINISHED BLOCK SIZE: 15" x 15"
Designed and pieced by Kim Diehl. Machine quilted by Deborah Poole.

Piecing the Blocks

Sew all pieces with right sides together using a ¼" seam allowance unless otherwise noted.

1. Join assorted print 1½" x 3½" A rectangles to opposite sides of a red 3½" square. Press the seam allowances toward the rectangles. Stitch and press an assorted print 1½" x 5½" B rectangle to the remaining sides of the red square. Press the seam allowances toward the rectangles. Continue adding rectangles to the pieced square in alphabetical order as shown to build the log-cabin unit, pressing the seam allowances away from the center square. Repeat for a total of 33 pieced log-cabin units measuring 9½" square, including the seam allowances.

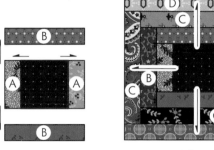
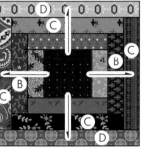

Make 33.

2. Stitch each light-brown triangle to a dark-tan triangle along the long diagonal edges. Press the seam allowances toward the light-brown triangles. Trim away the dog-ear points.

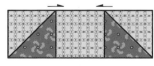

Make 72.

3. Join half-square-triangle units to opposite sides of a dark-tan 3½" square. Press the seam allowances toward the dark-tan square. Repeat for a total of 36 pieced triangle units.

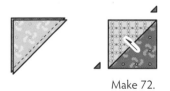

Make 36.

4. Join pieced triangle units from step 3 to opposite sides of a pieced log-cabin unit from step 1. Press the seam allowances toward the log-cabin unit. Repeat for a total of nine pieced block segments. Reserve the remaining pieced log-cabin units for use in the border.

Make 9.

6. Join pieced square units from step 5 to the ends of a remaining pieced triangle unit from step 3. Press the seam allowances toward the pieced square units. Repeat for a total of 18 pieced units.

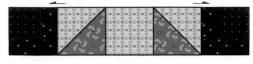

Make 18.

7. Join pieced units from step 6 to the remaining sides of the block segments from step 4. Press the seam allowances toward the log-cabin block centers. Repeat for a total of nine pieced blocks measuring 15½" square, including the seam allowances.

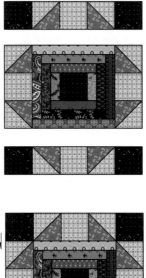

Make 9.

5. Join a chocolate-brown 1½" x 2½" rectangle to a red 2½" square. Press the seam allowances toward the brown rectangle. Join a chocolate-brown 1½" x 3½" rectangle to the bottom of the unit. Press the seam allowances toward the brown rectangle. Repeat for a total of 36 pieced square units.

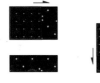

Make 36.

Piecing the Quilt Center

1. Using the quilt photo on page 64 as a guide, lay out four light-tan 1½" x 15½" strips and three pieced blocks in alternating positions, turning every other block to alternate the placement of the log-cabin strips. Join the pieces. Press the seam allowances toward the tan strips. Repeat for a total of three pieced block rows.

2. Lay out four chocolate-brown 1½" squares and three light-tan 1½" x 15½" strips in alternating positions. Join the pieces. Press the seam allowances toward the tan strips. Repeat for a total of four pieced sashing rows.

3. Referring to the quilt photo, lay out the pieced sashing rows and pieced block rows in alternating positions. Join the rows. Press the seam allowances toward the sashing rows. The pieced quilt center should now measure 49½" square, including the seam allowances.

Assembling and Adding the Border

1. Lay out five reserved log-cabin units to form a row, turning every other block to alternate the placement of the log-cabin strips. Join the blocks. Press the seam allowances toward the blocks with the long side strips and no seams. Join an assorted print 1½" x 9½" strip to each end of the pieced row. Press the seam allowances toward the newly added strips. Repeat for a total of four pieced strips.

Make 4.

2. Join a light-tan 1½" x 9½" strip to each short end of a pieced strip. Press the seam allowances away from the tan strips. Repeat for a total of four pieced border strips. Join two of these pieced strips to the right and left sides of the quilt center. Press the seam allowances toward the light-tan sashing strips.

Make 4.

3. Using the quilt photo as a guide for placement, join a pieced log-cabin unit to each end of the remaining pieced strips from step 2. Press the seam allowances toward the light-tan strips. Join these pieced strips to the remaining sides of the quilt center. Press the seam allowances toward the light-tan sashing strips. The pieced quilt top should now measure 67½" square, including the seam allowances.

Completing the Quilt

Referring to "Finishing Techniques" on page 108 for any details needed, layer the quilt top, batting, and backing. Quilt the layers. The featured quilt was machine quilted with an overall swirling pattern as shown on page 110. Join the seven chocolate-brown 2½" x 42" strips into one length and use it to bind the quilt.

Wreath of Lilies

*S*mall-scale patchwork, blooming lilies stitched from scraps of wool, and sprays of French knot stems add a touch of upscale primitive charm to this framed mini-quilt.

FINISHED QUILT SIZE, UNFRAMED: 8½" x 10½"

Designed, pieced, hand appliquéd, and hand quilted by Kim Diehl.

Materials

8 chubby sixteenths (9" x 11") of assorted tan prints for background

1 fat quarter (18" x 22") of brown print for stems, star-unit patchwork, and binding

16 squares, 1½" x 1½", of assorted prints for flying-geese patchwork

8 squares, 1" x 1", of assorted prints for star-unit patchwork

4 squares, approximately 2½" x 2½", of assorted cranberry wools for lily appliqués

8 rectangles, approximately 2" x 3", of assorted green wools for leaf appliqués

4 squares, approximately 2" x 2", of assorted blue wools for lily appliqués

Scraps of assorted orange wools for berry appliqués

1 fat quarter of fabric for backing

1 fat quarter of complimentary print for framed quilt background

14" x 16" rectangle of batting

Approximately ½ yard of HeatnBond lite iron-on adhesive

Fine-tip water-soluble marker

8 or #12 perle cotton (I used Valdani's #12 variegated perle cotton in H212 Faded Brown)

Size 5 embroidery needle

Bias bar to fit your stems

8 small assorted buttons

14" x 17" frame with 10½" x 13½" opening

11" x 14" piece of foam core board

Acid-free spray adhesive

Appliqué supplies (see page 99)

Cutting

Cut all pieces across the width of the fabric in the order given unless otherwise noted. Refer to "Cutting Bias Strips" on page 96 to cut bias strips. For greater ease in preparation, cutting instructions are provided separately for the appliqués.

From the 8 of assorted tan prints, cut a *combined total* of:

12 strips, 1" x 8½"

From the remainder of *each* of 2 of the tan prints, cut (for the star side-point units):

2 strips, 1" x 4" (combined total of 4)

From the remainder of *each* of 2 of the remaining tan prints, cut (for the star top- and bottom-point units):

2 strips, 1" x 4" (combined total of 4)

1 rectangle, 1" x 1½" (combined total of 2)

From the remainder of *each* of the last 4 remaining tan prints, cut:

1 strip, 1" x 11" (combined total of 4)

From the brown print, cut:

2 binding strips, 2½" x 22"

1 square, 1½" x 1½"

4 *bias* strips, 1" x 4"

Piecing the Quilt Top

Sew all pieces with right sides together using a ¼" seam allowance unless otherwise noted.

1. Using the tan 1" x 4" strips for the star side-point units, join one of each print along the long edges. Press the seam allowances open. Repeat with the remaining two strips cut from these prints.

Make 2.

2. Draw a diagonal line from corner to corner on the wrong side of each assorted print 1" and 1½" square.

3. Layer a prepared 1" square over one corner of a pieced strip from step 1 as shown. Stitch the pieces together along the drawn line. Referring to "Pressing Triangle Units" on page 98, press and trim the unit to make a star point. In the same manner, stitch, press, and trim a second prepared square onto the adjacent corner of the pieced strip, positioning it to form a mirror-image star point. Repeat with the remaining pieced strip from step 1 to form a mirror-image unit, taking care to position the tan prints so they will run continuously across the top after the quilt has been pieced.

Make 1 unit and 1 mirror-image unit.

4. Join the pieced units from step 3 to opposite sides of the brown 1½" square to make the star center unit. Press the seam allowances toward the brown square.

5. Select a tan 1" x 1½" rectangle for the star top- and bottom-points unit and two prepared 1" squares. Refer to "Pressing Triangle Units" to make a star-point unit as shown. Repeat for a total of two star-point units.

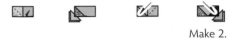

Make 2.

6. Join a matching tan 1" x 4" strip to each side of the star-point units from step 5 as shown. Press the seam allowances away from the pieced star-point units.

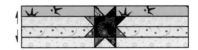

Make 2.

7. Stitch the pieced star-point units to the remaining sides of the star center unit from step 4. Press the seam allowances away from the star center.

8. Join six assorted tan 1" x 8½" strips along the long edges. Press the seam allowances in one direction. Repeat for a total of two pieced strip units. Join these units to the top and bottom edges of the star unit, ensuring the seam allowances are oriented away from the star. Press the seam allowances away from the star.

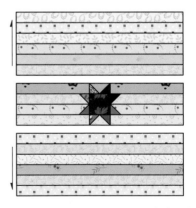

9. Select two assorted tan 1" x 11" strips. Join the pair along the long edges to make a strip set. Press the seam allowances to one side. Repeat to make a total of two pieced strip sets. Crosscut *each* strip set into three segments, 2½" wide, and two segments, 1½" wide.

Make 2 strip sets.
Cut *each* into 3 segments, 2½" wide,
and 2 segments, 1½" wide.

10. Select two prepared assorted print 1½" squares from step 2 and a 2½"-wide strip-set segment. Follow step 5 to make a pieced flying-geese unit. Repeat for a total of six pieced flying-geese units.

Make 6.

11. Layer a prepared assorted print 1½" square over a 1½"-wide strip-set segment as shown. Stitch the pair together along the drawn line. Press and trim as previously instructed. Repeat to make a mirror-image half-square-triangle unit. Repeat to make a total of four half-square-triangle units.

Make 2 each.

12. Lay out three pieced flying-geese units and the mirror-image half-square-triangle units stitched from the same tan prints as shown. Join the pieces. Press the seam allowances to one side, choosing the side that will result in the best point. Repeat for a total of two pieced flying-geese strips.

Make 2.

13. Join the tan-print sides of the pieced flying-geese strips to the top and bottom edges of the pieced quilt top. Press the seam allowances away from the flying-geese units. The pieced quilt top should now measure 8½" x 10½", including the seam allowances.

Preparing and Stitching the Wool Appliqués

1. Referring to "Preparing Wool Appliqués" on page 106 and using the appliqué patterns on page 73, trace and prepare the appliqués from the wool colors indicated in "Materials" on page 69.

2. Referring to "Making Bias-Tube Stems and Vines" on page 102, prepare the stems from the brown bias strips. Turn under one end of each prepared stem, apply a small amount of fabric glue stick, and heat set the stem from the back to result in stems that each have one finished end.

3. Referring to "Stitching Wool Appliqués" on page 107, stitch the blue wool band onto each lily.

4. Reverse the pattern sheet to use as a placement guide. Using the pattern sheet and the quilt photo for placement, lay out the prepared stems, lilies, and leaves. When you are pleased with the placement and everything fits to your liking, baste the appliqués in place, tucking the raw ends of the wool leaves underneath the stems. Use your favorite appliqué method to stitch the stems in place. (I hand stitched my stems with matching thread and a size 9 straw needle.) Stitch the wool appliqués in place. Last, position, baste, and stitch the berries.

5. Using the fine-tip water-soluble marker and referring to the placement guide as needed, draw stems radiating out from each lily stem, between the outer leaf and the lily. Use a single strand of perle cotton and a size 5 embroidery needle to stem stitch the drawn stems and add sprays of randomly placed French knots.

   Note: If your tan prints are sheer enough that there's a chance you'll see a shadowing effect from the perle cotton used to form the French knots, you can carefully add these after the quilt top has been layered with the batting and backing and quilted. Simply slide the needle through the layers as you travel from knot to knot, and bury the thread tails between the layers.

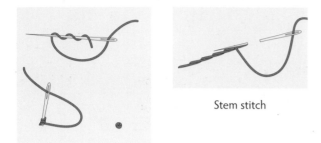

French knot

Stem stitch

Completing the Quilt

1. Referring to "Finishing Techniques" on page 108 for any necessary details, layer the quilt top, batting, and backing. Quilt the layers. The featured quilt was hand quilted in the ditch (along the seam lines) of the patchwork, and the appliqués were outline quilted to emphasize their shape.

2. Join the two brown 2½"-wide strips into one length and use it to bind the quilt.

3. Referring to the quilt photo for placement, stitch the buttons to the dark triangles at the top and bottom edges of the quilt top, knotting the thread on top of each button and leaving a decorative thread tail.

PIN POINT

Framing the Quilt

Framing this little quilt is a snap to do. Measure the opening of the frame from the back and use an old rotary cutter and acrylic ruler to trim the foam core board very slightly smaller than this measured size (just a thread's width or two along each side). Then spray the foam core board with adhesive and apply the fat quarter of complementary print, centering it and smoothing away any wrinkles. From the back, use a rotary cutter to trim away the excess fabric around the perimeter of the board. Next, center the quilt onto the front of the board and use masking tape to anchor it while securing the quilt in place. Last, use a hammer to tap the tip of an embroidery needle through each corner of the quilt, and also at approximately the center position of each long side. Use these holes to tap a threaded embroidery needle (with thread to match the binding) through each opening from the back, bringing it to the back again near the original hole and securely knotting the threads, leaving a generous tail. Place the mounted quilt into the frame (minus the glass), attach the backing piece, and enjoy!

Appliqué patterns do not include seam allowances. Asymmetrical shapes will appear reversed after stitching.

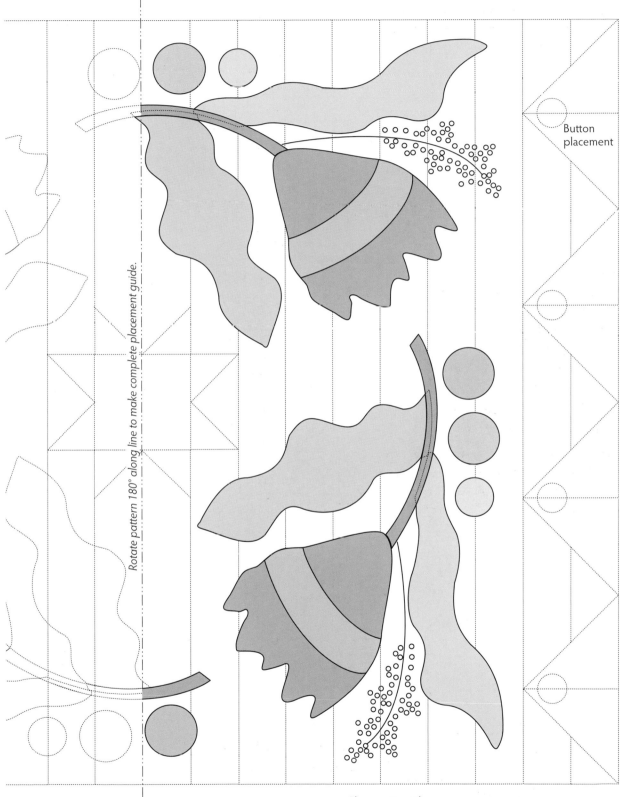

Rotate pattern 180° along line to make complete placement guide.

Button
placement

Placement guide

Mending Basket

*G*ather a plethora of prints,
enjoy getting back to basics,
and dive into some fun as you piece
this scrappy patchwork project.
Full of old-fashioned appeal, you'll
dream sweet dreams under this
quilt for many nights to come.

Materials

11 fat quarters (18" x 22") of assorted prints for
   block setting squares
19 fat eighths (9" x 22") of assorted prints for X units
18 fat eighths of assorted prints for pieced
   sashing strips
1⅞ yards of tan print for X units
⅔ yard of complementary print for binding
5 yards of fabric for backing
74" x 90" rectangle of batting

Cutting

*Cut all strips across the width of the fabric in the order
given unless otherwise noted.*

From the tan print, cut:
21 strips, 2⅞" x 42"; crosscut into 266 squares,
   2⅞" x 2⅞". Cut each square in half diagonally *once*
   to yield 532 triangles.

**From *each* of the 19 fat eighths of assorted prints
designated for the X units, cut:**
14 squares, 2⅞" x 2⅞"; cut each square in half
   diagonally *once* to yield 28 triangles (combined
   total of 532)
Keep the triangles organized by print.

**From *each* of the 18 fat eighths of assorted prints
designated for the pieced sashing strips, cut:**
12 rectangles, 2½" x 4½" (combined total of 216)

**From *each* of the 11 fat quarters of assorted
prints, cut:**
12 squares, 4½" x 4½" (combined total of 132)

From the complementary print, cut:
8 binding strips, 2½" x 42"

Piecing the Blocks

*Sew all pieces with right sides together using a ¼" seam
allowance unless otherwise noted.*

1. Select an assorted print triangle and a tan triangle. Stitch the pair together along the long
   diagonal edges. Press the seam allowances
   toward the assorted print triangle. Trim away the
   dog-ear points. Repeat for a total of 532 pieced
   half-square-triangle units measuring 2½" square,
   including the seam allowances. Keep the units
   organized by print for greater ease in assembling
   the blocks.

Make 133 sets of 4.

2. Select four pieced half-square-triangle units sewn
   from a matching print. Lay out the units in two
   horizontal rows of two units each as shown. Join
   the units in each row. Press the seam allowances
   open. Join the rows. Press the seam allowances
   open. Repeat for a total of seven pieced X units

"Mending Basket"

FINISHED QUILT SIZE: 68½" x 84½"

FINISHED BLOCK SIZE: 12" x 12"

Designed by Kim Diehl. Pieced by Pat Peyton. Machine quilted by Deborah Poole.

Perfect Triangles

My friend Pat shared a great tip with me that she used as she was piecing the half-square-triangle units for this quilt, and it's such an excellent idea that I feel it's worth passing on. After cutting her fabrics, Pat chose one perfectly cut triangle and taped it to a square of paper, which she then kept at her sewing machine. As she was layering her triangles together for stitching, she used this triangle template to check the size of any layered pairs that didn't match up perfectly. Comparing triangles that seemed "off" in size to this template enabled her to see possible discrepancies and made it easy to adjust her piecing accordingly to compensate. Neat trick!

from *each* of the 19 assorted prints (combined total of 133) measuring 4½" square, including the seam allowances.

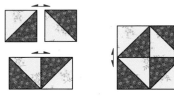

Make 133.

3. Lay out five pieced X units and four assorted print 4½" setting squares in three horizontal rows as shown. Join the pieces in each row. Press the seam allowances toward the setting squares. Join the rows. Press the seam allowances toward the middle row. Repeat for a total of 16 pieced A blocks measuring 12½" square, including the seam allowances.

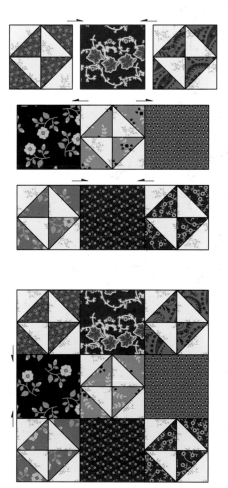

Block A.
Make 16.

4. Lay out four pieced X units and five assorted print 4½" setting squares in three horizontal rows as shown. Join the pieces in each row. Press the seam allowances toward the setting squares. Join the rows. Press the seam allowances away from the middle row. Repeat for a total of 12 pieced B blocks measuring 12½" square, including the seam allowances. Please note that you'll have five unused X units and eight unused setting squares; these have been included for added versatility as you piece the blocks.

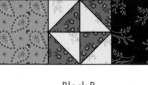

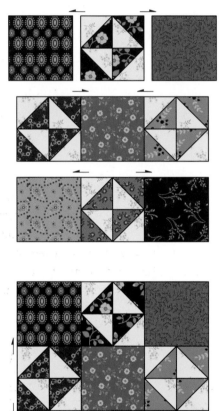

Block B.
Make 12.

Piecing the Sashing Strips

1. Select two assorted print 2½" x 4½" rectangles. Join the pair along the long edges. Press the seam allowances to one side. Repeat for a total of 108 pieced sashing units measuring 4½" square, including the seam allowances.

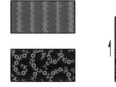

Make 108.

2. Join three pieced sashing units as shown on page 79. Press the seam allowances away from the middle unit. Repeat for a total of 35 pieced sashing strips measuring 4½" x 12½", including the seam allowances. Please note that you'll have

three unused units; these have been included for added versatility as you piece the strips.

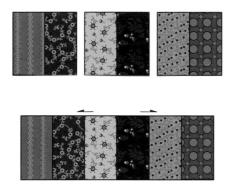

Make 35.

Piecing the Quilt Top

1. Lay out five pieced sashing strips and four A blocks in alternating positions as shown. Join the pieces. Press the seam allowances toward the sashing strips. Repeat for a total of four pieced A rows measuring 12½" x 68½", including the seam allowances.

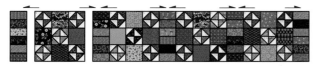

Row A.
Make 4.

PIN POINT

Easily Transporting Patchwork Units

Many of us use flannel-backed tablecloth fabric that's been cut into squares to help keep our in-progress patchwork and appliqué blocks organized as we work with them, but Pat took the idea one step further for this project. After arranging her patchwork row units on a design wall, she used a 12" width-of-fabric strip cut from a tablecloth remnant (with the flannel side up) and used it to transport her pieces to her sewing machine. This flannel strip enabled Pat to keep her pieces positioned in her arranged order as she moved them, and it eliminated the need for a lot of fussing, pinning, and labeling. Clever!

2. Lay out five pieced sashing strips and four pieced B blocks in alternating positions as shown. Join the pieces. Press the seam allowances toward the sashing strips. Repeat for a total of three pieced B rows measuring 12½" x 68½", including the seam allowances.

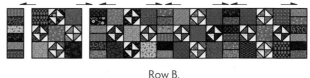

Row B.
Make 3.

3. Referring to the quilt photo on page 76, lay out the pieced A and B rows in alternating positions. Join the rows. Press the seam allowances toward the B rows. The pieced quilt top should now measure 68½" x 84½", including the seam allowances.

Completing the Quilt

Referring to "Finishing Techniques" on page 108 for any details needed, layer the quilt top, batting, and backing. Quilt the layers. The featured quilt was machine quilted with an overall crosshatch design for an old-fashioned feel. Join the eight complementary print 2½" x 42" strips into one length and use it to bind the quilt.

*L*ong on casual appeal and short on sewing time, this machine-appliquéd quilt with a touch of Americana flair can be stitched in a snap. Big-stitch hand quilting adds the perfect finish for a serving of homestyle charm.

Materials

2⅞ yards of neutral stripe or print for background*

26 chubby sixteenths (9" x 11") of assorted prints for four-patch units and binding

1⅓ yards of navy-blue print for outer border and yo-yo star centers

½ yard of gold print for large leaf appliqués

⅓ yard of red print for inner border and star appliqués

1 fat quarter (18" x 22") of green print for small leaf appliqués

3½ yards of fabric for backing

66" x 66" square of batting

#8 or #12 perle cotton (I used Valdani's #12 variegated perle cotton in H212 Faded Brown)

Size 5 embroidery needle

Freezer paper

Appliqué supplies (see page 99)

If your print is wide enough to be able to cut a 44½" square, you can reduce this amount to 1⅝ yards.

Cutting

Cut all pieces across the width of the fabric in the order given unless otherwise noted. Refer to page 85 for the yo-yo pattern and appliqué patterns A–C and to "Invisible Machine Appliqué" beginning on page 99 for pattern piece preparation.

From the *lengthwise grain* of the neutral stripe or print, cut:

2 rectangles, 22½" x 44½"

4 squares, 8½" x 8½"

From *each* of the 26 assorted prints, cut:

3 squares, 2¾" x 2¾" (combined total of 78)

1 binding strip, 2½" x 11" (combined total of 26)

From the red print, cut:

5 strips, 1½" x 42"

10 stars using pattern A

From the gold print, cut:

12 large leaves using pattern B

12 reversed large leaves using pattern B

From the green print, cut:

8 small leaves using pattern C

8 reversed small leaves using pattern C

From the *lengthwise grain* of the navy-blue print, cut:

4 strips, 7½" x 44½"

From the remainder of the navy-blue print, cut:

10 circles using the yo-yo pattern

Piecing the Four-Patch Units

Sew all pieces with right sides together using a ¼" seam allowance unless otherwise noted.

Select four assorted print 2¾" squares. Lay out the squares in two horizontal rows of two squares each as shown on page 83. Join the squares in each row. Press the seam allowances in opposite directions. Join the rows. Press the seam allowances in one direction. Repeat to make a total of 19 pieced four-patch units measuring 6" square, including the seam

"Starberry Jam"
FINISHED QUILT SIZE: 60½" x 60½"

*Designed, pieced, and machine appliquéd by Kim Diehl. Machine quilted
by Deborah Poole with hand-quilted accents by Kim Diehl.*

allowances. Please note that you'll have two unused 2¾" squares; these have been included for added versatility as you piece the four-patch units.

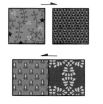

Make 19.

Piecing and Appliquéing the Quilt Center

1. Join the two neutral stripe or print 22½" x 44½" rectangles along the long edges to make a pieced background square. Press the seam allowances open. Please note that if you were able to cut a 44½" square from your background print, you can skip this step.

2. From freezer paper, use a rotary cutter and an acrylic ruler to cut 19 squares, 5½" x 5½". (To simplify this process, I stacked several layers of freezer paper together, anchored them with a straight pin, and cut multiple squares at once.) Fold each freezer-paper square in half and finger-press a center vertical crease; refold in the opposite direction to press a horizontal crease.

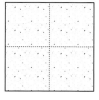

Make 19.

3. Apply a small amount of fabric glue stick to the dull paper side of a prepared freezer-paper square. On the wrong side of a four-patch unit, align the creases of the freezer-paper square, shiny side up, and press it into place with your hands. Referring to "Pressing Appliqués" on page 101, prepare the appliqué edges for stitching. Repeat with the remaining freezer-paper squares and pieced four-patch units.

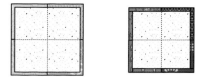

4. Measure 16" outward from each side of the center seam of the pieced background square and use a hot, dry iron to press a vertical crease from top to bottom. (If you used a whole square for your background, first fold the square in half and press a center vertical crease.) Refold the background square in the opposite direction and press a center horizontal crease.

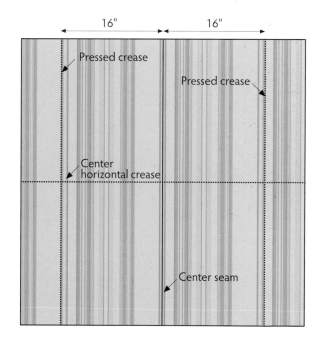

5. Beginning with the intersection of the vertical center seam or crease and the horizontal crease, lay out and glue baste a prepared four-patch appliqué, aligning the points with the background creases to perfectly center it. Work out from this center four-patch appliqué to glue baste and add two more four-patch appliqués above and below the center square, with the points just

touching, and resting them on the seam or crease to position them in a straight line.

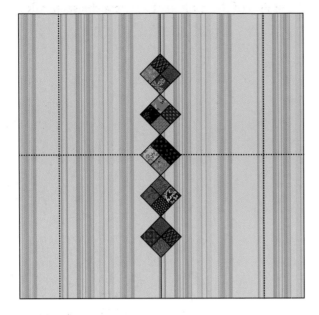

6. Repeat step 5 with the remaining four-patch appliqués and background creases to form three vertical four-patch columns. Referring to "Stitching Appliqués" on page 104, appliqué the four patches in place. Referring to "Removing Paper Pattern Pieces" on page 105, remove the paper pattern pieces. Reserve the remaining four-patch appliqués for use in the outer border.

7. Using the quilt photo as a guide, position and glue baste five prepared star appliqués in the open area between the center and left row of appliquéd four patches. Repeat with the remaining right-hand side of the quilt center. (Please note that I positioned the stars with the points placed randomly to eliminate having an obvious top or bottom to the finished quilt.) Next, position and glue baste two large leaf appliqués and two reversed large leaf appliqués radiating out from each star. Last, add the small leaf appliqués as shown in the quilt photo. Stitch the appliqués in place and remove the paper pattern pieces.

Stitching and Appliquéing the Yo-Yos

1. To make the yo-yo star centers, select a navy-blue yo-yo fabric circle. With the wrong side up, turn a portion of the edge toward you a scant ¼" to create a hem. Using a knotted length of perle cotton and an embroidery needle, bring the needle

up through the hem from the wrong side of the folded fabric to bury the knot between the layers. Sew a running stitch, with your stitches approximately ¼" in length, through all of the layers, near the folded edge. Continue turning the hem to the front and stitching as you work your way around the circle to your starting point; gently pull the threaded needle to gather the yo-yo edges into the center. Insert the needle under the gathered edge, just to the side of the center opening, and bring it out on the back of the yo-yo. Knot and clip the thread from the back, keeping the gathers taut. Repeat for a total of 10 stitched yo-yos.

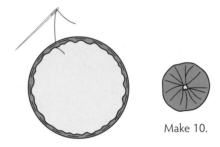

Make 10.

2. Glue baste and center a stitched yo-yo onto each star and appliqué it in place.

Appliquéing and Adding the Borders

1. Fold each neutral stripe or print 8½" square in half and use a hot, dry iron to press a vertical center crease. Refold the square in the opposite direction and press a horizontal center crease. Align the points of a reserved glue-basted four-patch appliqué with the pressed background creases. Use your hands to press the appliqué in place. Repeat with the remaining neutral squares and four-patch appliqués. Stitch the appliqués in place and remove the paper pattern pieces.

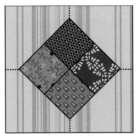

Make 4.

2. From one of the red 1½" x 42" strips, cut four segments, 3" wide. Join a segment to each remaining 1½" x 42" strip for a total of four pieced red strips. Press the seam allowances to one side.

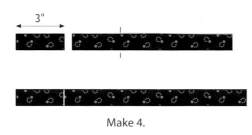

Make 4.

3. Join a pieced red strip to a navy-blue 7½" x 44½" strip. Press the seam allowances toward the red strip. Repeat with the remaining red and navy-blue strips.

4. Join the red edges of the pieced border strips to the right and left sides of the quilt center. Carefully press the seam allowances toward the red strips, taking care not to apply heat to the appliqués. Join an appliquéd neutral 8½" square to each end of the remaining pieced border

strips. Press the seam allowances away from the squares. Join these strips to the top and bottom edges of the quilt center. Press the seam allowances away from the quilt center. The completed quilt top should now measure 60½" square, including the seam allowances.

Completing the Quilt

Referring to "Finishing Techniques" on page 108 for any details needed, layer the quilt top, batting, and backing. Quilt the layers. The featured quilt was machine quilted along the stripes of the quilt-center background and straight lines were stitched onto the four-patch units, radiating out at regular intervals from the center seams. A straight line was quilted through the center of the red inner border, and a diagonal crosshatch was stitched onto the navy-blue outer border. To emphasize the appliqués, I used the big-stitch method (see page 109) to outline the shapes. Join the assorted print 2½" x 11" strips into one length and use it to bind the quilt.

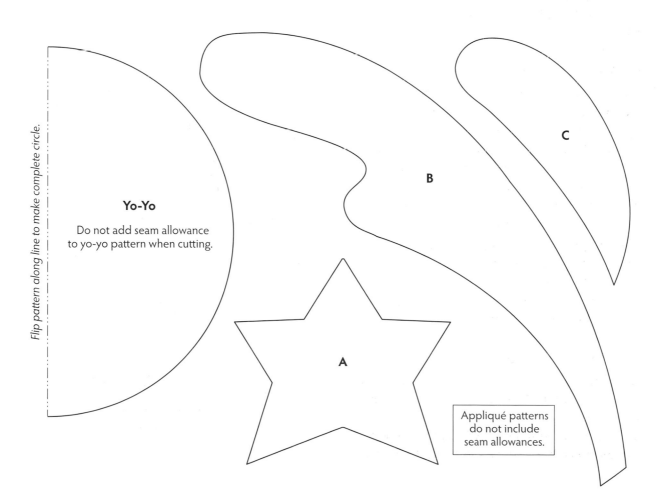

Flip pattern along line to make complete circle.

Yo-Yo

Do not add seam allowance to yo-yo pattern when cutting.

C

B

A

Appliqué patterns do not include seam allowances.

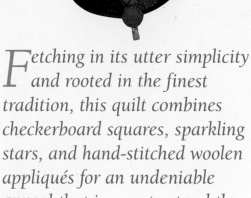

*F*etching in its utter simplicity and rooted in the finest tradition, this quilt combines checkerboard squares, sparkling stars, and hand-stitched woolen appliqués for an undeniable appeal that is sure to stand the test of time.

Materials

3¾ yards of neutral print for patchwork and appliqué backgrounds

3¼ yards of red print for center star and border patchwork

¾ yard of chocolate-brown print for center star patchwork and binding

1 fat eighth (9" x 22") of green stripe or print for stems

12 chubby sixteenths (9" x 11") of assorted prints for checkerboard patchwork

30 squares, 6" x 6", of assorted-color wools for penny stacks and tulip flower petals

4 rectangles, 6" x 10", of assorted green wools for large leaves

4 rectangles, 4½" x 8½", of assorted red wools for tulips

4 squares, 6" x 6", of assorted orange wools for oak leaves

4 squares, 6" x 6", of assorted gold wools for flowers and tulip bases

3 squares, 6" x 6", of assorted green wools for *small leaves*

4 squares, 6" x 6", of assorted blue wools for berries

4 yards of fabric for backing

70" x 70" square of batting

Approximately 2 yards of HeatnBond lite iron-on adhesive

#8 or #12 perle cotton (Kim used Valdani's #12 variegated perle cotton in H212 Faded Brown)

Size 5 embroidery needle

Bias bar to fit your stems

Appliqué supplies (see page 99)

Cutting

Cut all pieces across the width of the fabric in the order given unless otherwise noted. Refer to "Cutting Bias Strips" on page 96 to cut bias strips. For greater ease, cutting instructions for the appliqués are provided separately.

From the chocolate-brown print, cut:

1 strip, 4½" x 42"; crosscut into:

   1 square, 4½" x 4½"

   8 squares, 2½" x 2½"

7 binding strips, 2½" x 42"

From the neutral print, cut:

23 strips, 2½" x 42"; crosscut into:

   4 rectangles, 2½" x 4½"

   354 squares, 2½" x 2½"

5 strips, 4½" x 42"; crosscut into 36 squares, 4½" x 4½"

2 strips, 10½" x 42"; crosscut into 4 squares, 10½" x 10½"*

2 strips, 10½" x 42"; crosscut into 4 rectangles, 10½" x 16½"

*If your fabrics haven't been prewashed, you may be able to cut all four squares from one width-of-fabric strip.

From the red print, cut:

2 strips, 4½" x 42"; crosscut into:

   4 rectangles, 4½" x 8½"

   4 squares, 4½" x 4½"

2 strips, 8½" x 42"; crosscut into 8 squares, 8½" x 8½"

21 strips, 2½" x 42"; crosscut into:

   112 rectangles, 2½" x 4½"

   112 squares, 2½" x 2½"

Continued on page 89

"Farm-Girl Finery"

FINISHED QUILT SIZE: 64½" x 64½"

FINISHED QUILT CENTER SIZE: 36" x 36"

Designed, pieced, machine appliquéd, and hand appliquéd by Kim Diehl.
Machine quilted by Deborah Poole.

Continued from page 87

From the *bias* of the green stripe or print, cut:
12 strips, 1¼" x 5"

From *each* of the 12 assorted prints, cut:
11 squares, 2½" x 2½" (combined total of 132)

Preparing the Appliqués

Appliqué patterns A–H are provided on pages 93–95. Referring to "Preparing Wool Appliqués" on page 106, and using the wool colors suggested in "Materials" on page 87 as a guide, prepare the following wool appliqués.

29 large pennies using pattern A
29 medium pennies using pattern B
29 small pennies using pattern C
4 flowers using pattern D
4 large flower centers using pattern B
4 small flower centers using pattern C
4 oak leaves using pattern E
12 small leaves using pattern F
12 tulip petals using pattern F
4 tulips using pattern G
4 round tulip bases using pattern C
4 large leaves using pattern H
4 reversed large leaves using pattern H
36 blueberries using pattern C

Appliquéing the Center-Star Penny Square

1. Referring to "Stitching Wool Appliqués" on page 107, work from the top layer to the bottom to stitch a penny stack consisting of one each of assorted wool A, B, and C pieces. Repeat for a total of 29 stacks.

2. Center, glue baste, and stitch one penny stack to the center of the chocolate-brown print 4½" square. Reserve the remaining stacks for later use.

Piecing the Double-Star Medallion Unit

Sew all pieces with right sides together using a ¼" seam allowance unless otherwise noted.

1. Using a pencil and an acrylic ruler, draw a diagonal line from corner to corner on the wrong side of each chocolate-brown 2½" square and each neutral 4½" square.

2. Layer a prepared brown square over one end of a neutral 2½" x 4½" rectangle. Stitch the pair together on the drawn line. Referring to "Pressing Triangle Units" on page 98, press and trim the stitched pair. Repeat for a total of four pieced rectangle units. In the same manner, use a prepared brown square to stitch a mirror-image point onto each pieced rectangle unit. Reserve the prepared neutral squares for later use.

Make 4.

3. Lay out the brown 4½" penny square from step 2 of "Appliquéing the Center-Star Penny Square," the four star-point units, and four neutral 2½" squares in three horizontal rows to form the brown center-star unit. Join the pieces in each row. Press the seam allowances away from the star-point units. Join the rows. Press the seam allowances away from the middle row. The pieced and appliquéd brown star unit should now measure 8½" square, including the seam allowances.

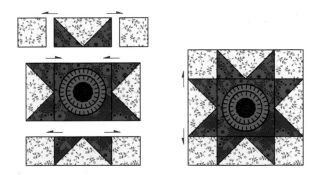

4. Using the reserved prepared neutral 4½" squares and four red print 4½" x 8½" rectangles, repeat step 2 to make four pieced neutral star-point units.

5. Referring to the quilt photo, lay out the four pieced neutral star-point units, four red print 4½" squares, and the pieced brown star unit from step 3 in three horizontal rows as shown. Join the pieces in each horizontal row. Press the seam allowances away from the star-point units. Join the rows. Press the seam allowances away from the middle row. The pieced double-star medallion unit should now measure 16½" square, including the seam allowances.

Piecing the Red Star-Point Units

1. Using a pencil and an acrylic ruler, draw a diagonal line from corner to corner on the wrong side of each red print 8½" square.

2. Using the prepared squares and neutral 10½" x 16½" rectangles, repeat step 2 of "Piecing the Double-Star Medallion Unit" to make four pieced red star-point units measuring 10½" x 16½", including the seam allowances.

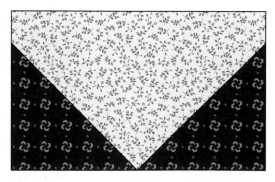

Make 4.

PIN POINT

"Unsewing" Diagonal Seams

When I discover that I've made a piecing error and need to "unsew" a diagonal seam, I first give it a quick spritz of Best Press starch alternative and then press it with a hot iron. This helps stabilize the fabrics and makes it possible to remove the stitching without distorting the patchwork pieces.

Appliquéing the Tulip Units

1. Referring to "Making Bias-Tube Stems and Vines" on page 102, prepare the green bias 1¼" x 5" stems.

2. With right sides together, fold each pieced red star-point unit in half and use a hot, dry iron to press a center vertical crease.

3. Using the quilt photo on page 88 as a guide and the pressed crease for centering, lay out one prepared stem, one tulip, one large leaf, and one reversed large leaf, ensuring the raw edges of the leaves rest under the center of the stem at the pressed crease of the star-point unit. When you're pleased with the design, apply small dots of liquid basting glue to the rim of adhesive on the wrong side of the large leaves and anchor them in place. Remove the remaining pieces. Heat set the leaves from the back. Stitch the leaves to the background.

4. Reposition, glue baste, and heat set the stem, covering the raw ends of the large leaves. Use your favorite appliqué method to stitch the stem in place. (I used my invisible machine appliqué method to stitch the stems as outlined in "Stitching Appliqués" on page 104.)

5. Using the quilt photo as a guide, stitch three assorted-color F appliqué pieces onto the tulip to form petals.

prepared stems, three small leaves, and six berries onto one prepared neutral 10½" square, ensuring the stem ends are positioned approximately ¼" underneath the flower; trim away any excess stem length as needed to achieve the look you desire. When you're pleased with the design, glue baste the stems and heat set to anchor them in place. Remove the remaining pieces. Stitch the stems to the background.

4. Position, glue baste, heat set, and stitch the appliqués listed in step 3 to the square.

5. Repeat steps 3 and 4 for a total of four appliquéd flower squares.

Piecing the Star Medallion Unit

Referring to the quilt photo, lay out the center star unit, four appliquéd tulip units, and four appliquéd flower squares in three horizontal rows. Join the units in each row. Press the seam allowances away from the tulip units. Join the rows. Press the seam allowances away from the middle row. The pieced center-star medallion unit should now measure 36½" square, including the seam allowances.

Piecing and Adding the Checkerboard Border

1. Sew a neutral 2½" square to one of the assorted print 2½" squares. Press the seam allowances toward the assorted print square. Repeat for a total of 84 pieced pairs.

Make 84.

2. Join a neutral print 2½" square to the assorted print square of a pieced pair from step 1. Press the seam allowances toward the assorted print square. Repeat for a total of 42 A units.

Unit A.
Make 42.

6. Reposition, glue baste, heat set, and stitch the tulip unit onto the background, as well as three blueberries, ensuring the raw edges of the stem are overlapped approximately ¼". Last, position, glue baste, heat set, and stitch a gold penny circle onto the bottom of the tulip to cover the petal tips and overlap onto the stem.

7. Repeat steps 3–6 to appliqué a total of four tulip units.

Appliquéing the Flower Corner Squares

1. With right sides together, fold each neutral print 10½" square in half diagonally and use a hot, dry iron to press a diagonal crease from point to point.

2. Referring to "Appliquéing the Center-Star Penny Square" on page 89, layer and stitch four penny stacks consisting of a small and medium penny.

3. Using the quilt photo as a guide and the pressed diagonal crease for centering, lay out one flower, one penny stack from step 2, one oak leaf, two

3. Join an assorted print 2½" square to the neutral square of a pieced pair from step 1. Press the seam allowances toward the assorted print square. Repeat for a total of 42 B units. Please note that you'll have 6 unused assorted print squares; these have been included for added versatility as you stitch your patchwork.

Unit B.
Make 42.

4. Lay out nine A units and nine B units in alternating positions, beginning with an A unit, to form the checkerboard border. Join the units. Press the seam allowances toward the B units. Repeat for a total of two pieced rows. Join these rows to the right and left sides of the quilt center. Press the seam allowances toward the quilt center.

A   B

5. Referring to step 4, use 12 A units and 12 B units to make a checkerboard row. Repeat for a total of two pieced rows. Join these rows to the top and bottom edges of the quilt center. Press the seam allowances away from the checkerboard toward the quilt center.

A   B

Appliquéing, Piecing, and Adding the Outer Star Border

1. Referring to "Appliquéing the Center-Star Penny Square" on page 89, center and baste a reserved penny stack onto a neutral print 4½" square; stitch in place. Repeat for a total of 28 penny squares.

2. Using a pencil and an acrylic ruler, draw a diagonal line from corner to corner on the wrong side of the remaining neutral print 2½" squares.

3. Referring to step 2 of "Piecing the Double-Star Medallion Unit" on page 89, use the prepared neutral print 2½" squares and 112 red 2½" x 4½" rectangles to stitch 112 pieced star-point units.

4. Referring to step 3 of "Piecing the Double-Star Medallion Unit" on page 89, use one stitched penny square from step 1, four star-point units from step 3, and four red 2½" squares to stitch a Star block. Repeat for a total of 28 Star blocks measuring 8½" square, including the seam allowances.

5. Lay out six star units end to end. Join the units. Press the seam allowances open. Repeat for a total of two pieced star borders. Join these borders to the right and left sides of the quilt top. Next, lay out eight star units end to end. Join the units. Press the seam allowances open. Repeat for a total of two pieced star borders. Join these borders to the remaining sides of the quilt top. The completed quilt top should now measure 64½" square, including the seam allowances.

Completing the Quilt

Referring to "Finishing Techniques" on page 108 for any details needed, layer the quilt top, batting, and backing. Quilt the layers. The featured quilt was machine quilted with straight lines inside each pieced star to echo the shape. The red center star was stitched with a serpentine feathered vine. The neutral background of the center medallion was quilted with repeating straight lines radiating out from the red star. The checkerboard border was stitched with a crosshatch design, and feathered motifs were quilted onto the red portions of the outer star border. Last, the appliqués were outline quilted to emphasize their shapes. Join the seven brown 2½" x 42" strips into one length and use it to bind the quilt.

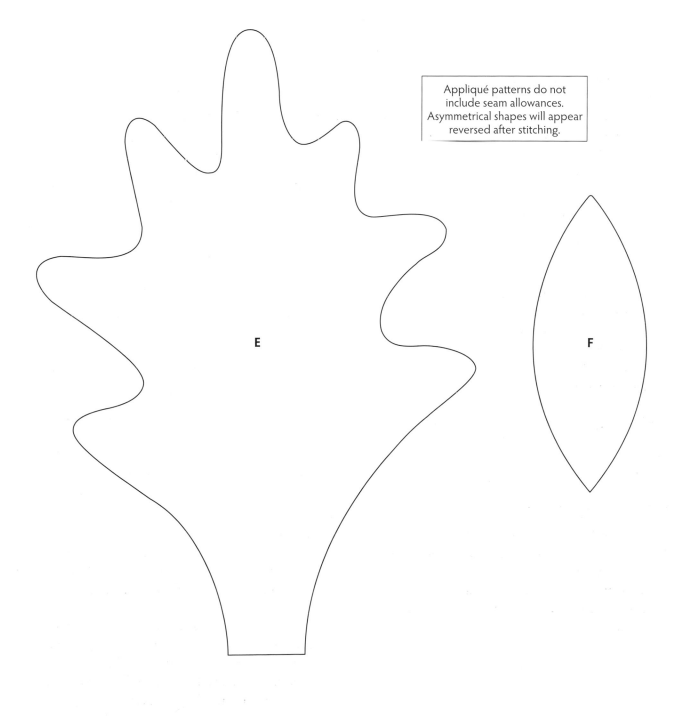

Appliqué patterns do not include seam allowances. Asymmetrical shapes will appear reversed after stitching.

E

F

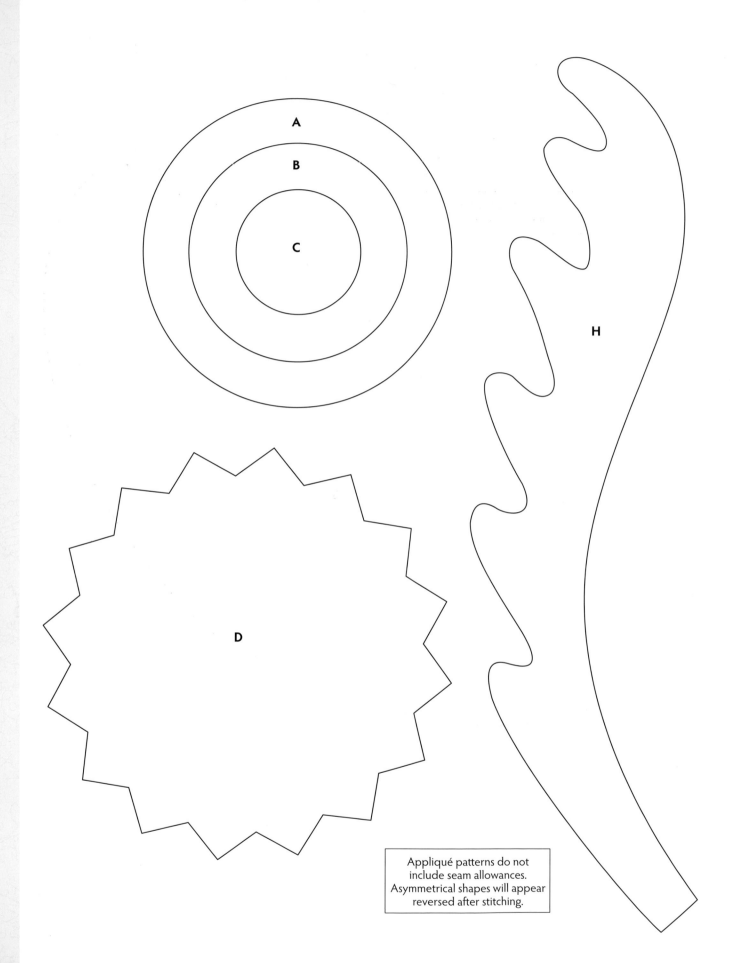

Appliqué patterns do not
include seam allowances.
Asymmetrical shapes will appear
reversed after stitching.

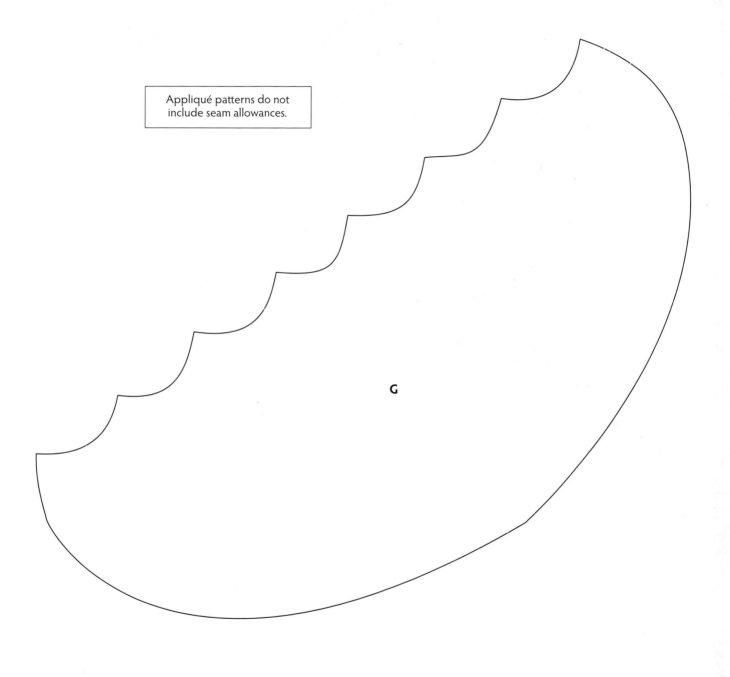

Appliqué patterns do not
include seam allowances.

G

Kim's Quiltmaking Basics

This section provides some great how-to information for the techniques and steps I use to make the quilts featured in my books.

For even more details and techniques, please visit ShopMartingale.com/HowtoQuilt, where you can download free illustrated guidelines.

Yardage Requirements

The project instructions in this book assume the following usable dimensions for yardage and precut pieces after prewashing and removing selvages: yardage, 42" width; fat quarter, 18" x 21"; fat eighth, 9" x 21"; chubby sixteenth, 9" x 10½". To make the best use of your fabric, always cut your pieces in the order given.

PIN POINT

Portable Patchwork Viewers

When I'm shopping for quilting fabrics, I've discovered that it can sometimes be difficult to look past the large scale of certain prints and envision them stitched into my patchwork. To help me see beyond the huge piece of fabric that's visible on the bolt, I often carry a recipe card in my purse with cutouts of 1" and 2" squares. Holding this "viewer" in front of the fabric lets me see a smaller peek of the print as it would appear in my patchwork and gives me a better perspective for how it will mingle and blend into my finished quilt.

Rotary Cutting

Unless otherwise noted, please cut all pieces on the straight of grain and across the width of the fabric. To speed the process of cutting my fabrics, I routinely fold my pressed fabric in half with the selvages together, and then in half once more. Folding the fabric in this way will result in four pieces with each cut. Of course, the number of folds you can make will be determined by the size of your patchwork.

Place the folded fabric on your cutting mat, aligning the folded edge with a horizontal line of the marked grid. Position your ruler on top of the fabric and make a vertical cut along one side to square it up and establish a straight edge. Measure and cut your pieces from this edge.

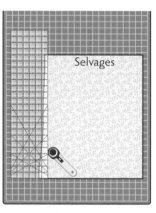

To cut half-square triangles from a square (or layered stack of squares), lay your ruler diagonally across the square with the cutting edge directly over the corners, and make the cut.

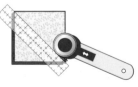

Cutting Bias Strips

Some projects in this book call for bias strips (lengths of cloth that have been cut diagonally rather than across the width of the fabric), which are usually used in projects that feature appliquéd stems and vines. The steps provided below are my preferred method for cutting these strips, as they enable me to work with a manageable size of cloth that produces strips approximately twice the cut length once they're unfolded. Another benefit of this method is that you can join the cut strips end to end to make one long length, and then cut the exact pieces you need from this joined strip, resulting in little or no waste.

1. After pressing the fabric smooth, lay it in a single layer on a large cutting mat. Grasp one corner of the fabric and fold it back to form a layered triangle of any size you choose, aligning the top straight edge with the straight grain of the bottom layer of fabric.

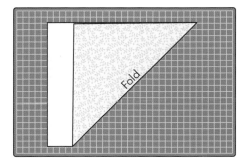

2. Rotate the layered pieced of cloth to align the folded edge with a cutting line on your mat, ensuring the fold is resting evenly along the marked line to prevent a "dog-leg" curve in your strips after they've been cut and unfolded.

3. Use an acrylic ruler and rotary cutter to cut through the folded edge of cloth a few inches in from one pointed end. With the ruler aligned with the lines of your cutting mat, begin cutting your strips at measured intervals from this edge (using the dimensions called for in your pattern instructions). If you reach the end of the folded edge of cloth and require additional strips, simply begin again at step 1 and repeat the process, using another corner of your cloth or squaring up the end from which you've been cutting.

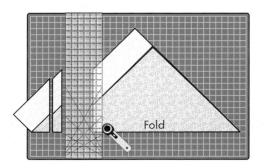

Fold

4. Square off the strip ends and trim them to the desired length, or sew multiple squared-off lengths together to achieve the length needed. Press the seam allowances to one side, all in the same direction. Experience has taught me that for strips which will be used for bias-tube stems, joining the lengths with straight seams (rather than diagonal seams that are traditionally used) will enable you to easily press the stems flat with a bias bar, as it will slide through the sewn tubes easily without becoming caught on the diagonal seams.

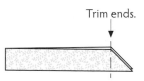

Trim ends.

Pinning

I recommend pinning your layered patchwork pieces together at regular intervals, including all sewn seams and intersections. A good tip for achieving a consistently sewn seam that extends to the back edge of your patchwork is to pin the pieces with glass-head pins; you can lay your fingertip over the pin heads and use them to steer the patchwork through the machine in a straight line, eliminating inaccurate seams at the back end of each piece where fishtailing often occurs.

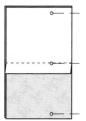

Machine Piecing

Unless otherwise instructed, always join your fabrics with right sides together using a ¼" seam allowance. To achieve an accurate seam allowance, I suggest using a ¼" presser foot made specifically for quilt-making. You can also easily make a sewing guide using masking tape. To do this, gently lower your sewing machine's needle until the point rests upon the ¼" line of an acrylic ruler. After ensuring that the ruler is resting in a straight position, apply a line of ¼" masking tape to the sewing-machine surface exactly along the ruler's edge, taking care not to cover the feed dogs. Align the edge of the fabrics with this taped line as you feed the pieces through the machine.

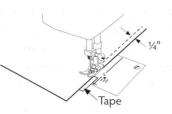

To achieve a crisp, clean look to my seams without visible stitches, and to achieve sewn seams that will remain intact all the way to the fabric edges, I routinely shorten my stitch length slightly to achieve more stitches to the inch. This shorter stitch length is especially helpful when piecing smaller-scale projects.

Chain Piecing

For projects with many pieces to be joined, chain piecing will save both time and thread. To chain piece, simply feed your patchwork units through the sewing machine one after another without snipping the threads between each. When you finish sewing the units, cut the threads connecting them and press as instructed.

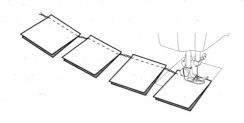

Pressing Seams

In my opinion, the benefits of pressing well are invaluable, as this step can affect the accuracy of your patchwork and the final appearance of your finished quilt. I recommend using a hot, dry iron and the following steps when pressing your seams.

1. Place the patchwork on a firm-surfaced ironing board with the fabric you wish to press toward (usually the darker hue) on top. On the wrong side of the fabric, briefly bring your iron down onto the sewn seam to warm the fabric.

2. Lift the iron and fold the top piece of fabric back to expose the right sides of the fabrics. While the fabric is still warm, run your fingernail along the sewn thread line to relax the fibers at the fold and open the cloth all the way to the line of

stitching. Press seam flat from the right side of the patchwork. The seam allowances will now lie under the fabric that was originally positioned on top.

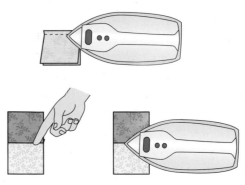

As a personal preference, I don't use steam when pressing my seams, because I find that using a dry iron enables me to easily modify my patchwork if an adjustment is needed. Once I've completed my patchwork unit or quilt top, I'll often give it a light steam press to set the seams more firmly in place and simplify the quilting process.

Pressing Triangle Units

Several projects in this book call for stitch-and-fold triangle units that are created by layering a square with a drawn diagonal line on top of a second square or rectangle. After stitching the pair together on the drawn line, I recommend the following steps.

1. Fold the top triangle back and align its corner with the corner of the bottom piece of fabric to keep it square; press in place.

2. Trim away the excess layers of fabric beneath the top triangle, leaving a ¼" seam allowance.

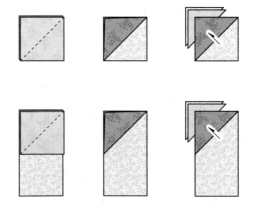

Traditionally, the seam allowances of triangle units are trimmed before they're pressed, but I've found that this pressing method produces more accurate patchwork that seldom requires squaring up.

Easily Stitching along Drawn Sewing Lines

Whenever my patchwork requires that I stitch along drawn sewing lines, such as stitch-and-fold triangle units, I remove my standard presser foot and snap on an open-toe foot for this step. Using an open-toe foot enables me to easily see my drawn lines during the stitching process, and greatly improves my accuracy for units that finish true to size.

Invisible Machine Appliqué

I love the results that can be achieved with my invisible machine appliqué method because it closely resembles the look of needle turn, and it's also a great time-saver. In addition to your standard quiltmaking supplies, the following tools and products are needed for this method:

- .004 monofilament thread in smoke and clear colors
- Awl or stiletto tool with a sharp point
- Bias bars in various widths
- Embroidery scissors with a fine, sharp point
- Freezer paper
- Iron with a sharp pressing point (travel-sized irons work especially well for this technique)
- Liquid basting glue, water-soluble and acid-free (my favorite brand is Quilter's Choice Basting Glue by Beacon Adhesives)
- Fabric glue stick
- Open-toe presser foot
- Pressing board with a *firm* surface
- Sewing machine with adjustable tension control, capable of producing a tiny zigzag stitch
- Size 75/11 (or smaller) machine-quilting needles
- Tweezers with rounded tips

Choosing Your Monofilament Thread

There are currently two types of monofilament thread (sometimes called "invisible thread") that work well for invisible machine appliqué: nylon and polyester. Both types have their own characteristics and strengths and can bring different benefits to your appliqué projects.

In my experience, nylon thread tends to produce results that are slightly less visible, but extra care should be used as your project is being assembled and pressed because this thread can be weakened by the heat of a very hot iron. For best results when working with nylon thread, avoid applying prolonged or high heat directly to the front of your appliqués and press any nearby seams with care. Once the project is finished and bound, I've found that the stitched appliqués will stand up well to everyday use and care. When I use nylon monofilament for my own projects, I've had very good results using the YLI brand.

If you'd like an extra measure of confidence that your appliqués will remain securely in place, even if they're inadvertently pressed from the front and exposed to direct heat from your iron, you may wish to use polyester monofilament thread. I find that the look of polyester monofilament can vary greatly from one brand to another, with some appearing less transparent or even shinier and heavier than others. Depending upon the brand you choose, the monofilament may be slightly more visible on your stitched appliqués. For projects where I've opted to use a polyester product, I've been very pleased with the Sulky brand, because I feel the results most closely resemble those that are achieved when using nylon.

Ultimately, I recommend that you experiment with both types of monofilament thread and make this decision based upon your own personal results and preferences.

Polarized Electrical Plugs

A neat little trick I've discovered to easily identify which side of my polarized plugs has the wider prong is to paint a small dab of brightly colored nail polish on the side of the plug with the wide piece. This spot of color makes it easy to tell at a glance which direction to hold the plug when inserting it into an outlet.

Preparing Pattern Templates

For projects featuring multiple appliqués made from one pattern, I've found that tracing around a sturdy template to make the number of pieces needed, rather than tracing over the pattern sheet numerous times, speeds the process tremendously and gives consistent results. Keep in mind as you make your templates that any shape can be modified to fit your skill level. And don't be afraid to fatten up thin tips or redraw narrow inner curves to plump them up and make the shapes more "friendly." Your resulting appliqués will look essentially the same, but your shapes will be much easier to work with.

Any time a pattern template is used, only one will be needed, as it will simply be a tool to enable you to easily make the individual freezer paper pattern pieces you'll use when preparing the appliqués. To make a sturdy paper template for tracing pattern pieces (which will eliminate the need to buy template plastic), use the steps that follow:

1. Cut a single piece of freezer paper about twice as large as your shape. Use a pencil to trace the pattern onto one end of the non-waxy side of the paper. Fold the freezer paper in half, waxy sides together, and use a hot, dry iron (I place mine on the "cotton" setting) to fuse the folded paper layers together.

2. Cut out the shape on the drawn line, taking care to duplicate it accurately.

Preparing Paper Pattern Pieces

Pattern *pieces* are used differently than pattern *templates*; pieces are individual paper shapes that you'll use as you prepare your appliqués from cloth. Always cut paper pattern pieces on the drawn lines; you'll add the seam allowances later as you cut your shapes from fabric. To achieve smooth pattern edges, I suggest moving the paper, rather than the scissors, as you take long cutting strokes.

Use the prepared template (or pattern sheet, if you're preparing fewer than a dozen pieces) to trace the specified number of pattern pieces onto the non-waxy side of a piece of freezer paper. To save time when many pieces are required, stack the freezer paper (up to eight layers deep for simple shapes, and four to six layers deep for more curvy or complex shapes) with the waxy sides facing down; anchor

them together using pins in the center of the shape to prevent shifting, or use staples at regular intervals slightly outside the shape in the background. Cut out the pattern pieces on the drawn lines, and discard the background areas.

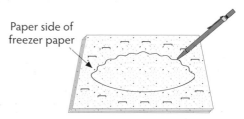

Paper side of freezer paper

Mirror-image pieces can easily be prepared by tracing the pattern onto the non-waxy side of one end of a strip of freezer paper, and then folding it accordion style in widths to fit your shape. Anchor the layers together as previously described and cut out the shape. When you separate the pieces, every other shape will be a mirror image.

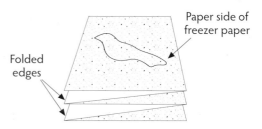

Paper side of freezer paper

Folded edges

I consistently use the accordion-fold technique for quickly making multiple pattern pieces of any shape that doesn't have an obvious direction, even if it isn't perfectly symmetrical, because this method speeds the process and adds interest to my finished quilt. Multiple pattern pieces for shapes that do have an obvious direction (such as a bird) should be prepared by stacking individual freezer-paper pieces waxy side down as described previously.

Preparing Appliqués

1. Apply a small amount of glue from a fabric glue stick to the center of the dull side of each paper pattern piece; affix it to the wrong side of your fabric with the shiny waxy side *up*, leaving approximately ½" between each shape for seam allowances. Experience has taught me that positioning the longest lines or curves of each shape on the diagonal is best, because the resulting bias edges are easier to work with than straight-grain

edges when pressing the seam allowances over onto the paper pattern pieces.

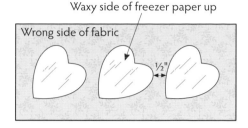

Waxy side of freezer paper up

Wrong side of fabric

½"

2. Using embroidery scissors, cut out each shape, adding an approximate ¼" seam allowance around the paper. For this technique, I've learned that more is actually better when it comes to seam allowances, as cutting too scant a seam allowance will make the fabric more difficult to handle and work with. As you work with each shape, any seam allowance section that feels too bulky can be trimmed a bit, but you can't make scant seam allowances bigger.

When turning seam allowances to the back of an appliqué to finish the edges, I've discovered that it's easier to press and prepare outer curves, straight edges, and outer points without clipping them. The seam allowances of inner points or pronounced inner curves should be clipped once at the center position, stopping two or three threads away from the paper edge and taking care not to clip into it. If you're unsure whether an inner curve is pronounced enough to need a clip, try pressing it without one—if the fabric easily follows the shape of the curve and lies flat, you've eliminated a step!

Clip inner points
to paper edge.

Pressing Appliqués

I suggest using the steps that follow to press the seam allowance of each appliqué, working at approximately the top edge of the shape on the side that's farthest away from you. As you follow these steps, always rotate the appliqué edge you're pressing toward the point of your iron as you work your way around the shape in one direction from start to finish. Working in one direction around each shape is important, because it will help the seam allowance at each point lie in the best position to achieve the crisp, sharp results we all want.

The smaller the shape or the curvier the edges are, the smaller the increments should be as you rotate and press your way around the piece—this will enable the fabric to smoothly hug the shape of your appliqué for flawless results. Always begin pressing along a straight edge or a gentle curve, never at a point or a corner, and rotate the appliqué toward the iron as previously suggested, because this will direct the seam allowance of any points toward your "smart" hand (which will later hold the awl or stiletto to fine-tune and finish any points).

1. Beginning at a straight or gently curved edge and working your way around the entire shape in one direction, use the pad of your finger to smooth the fabric seam allowance over onto the waxy side of the paper pattern piece, following with the point of a hot, dry iron (I place my iron on the "cotton" setting) and firmly pressing it in place. The weight of the iron will work together with the heat to anchor the seam to the pattern piece. To avoid puckered appliqué edges, always draw the seam allowance slightly backward toward the last section pressed. I routinely let the point of my iron rest on each newly pressed section of seam allowance, holding it in place as I draw the next section over onto the paper pattern piece. Allowing the iron to rest in place while you work will lengthen the amount of time the fabric receives heat, and it will help the cloth to stick more firmly to the paper.

Direct seam allowance
toward center of shape.

2. For sharp outer points, press the seam allowance so the folded edge of the fabric extends beyond the first side of the pattern point, snugging the fabric firmly up against the paper edge. Fold over the seam allowance of the remaining side of the point and continue pressing. After the seam allowance of the entire piece has been pressed, apply a small amount of glue stick to the bottom of the folded flap of fabric seam allowance at the point. If the seam allowance flap will be visible from the front of the appliqué, use the point of an awl or stiletto to drag the fabric in and away from the appliqué edge (not down from the point, as this will blunt it), and press the seam allowance flap with the point of a hot iron to heat set the glue and keep the flap in place. For narrow points, I like to roll the seam allowances under slightly as I draw them in from the edge with the awl; this will enable the seams to be completely hidden from the front of the appliqué.

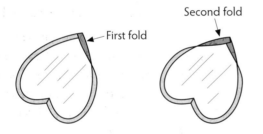

Second fold

First fold

One more tip I'd like to share to help achieve the beautiful sharp appliqué points we all strive for, is to ensure that your pressed seam allowance follows the line of the curve at the point, rather than the point itself. I've often found that when a point is less than perfect, it's because the seam allowance has flared out and away from the paper pattern piece. Following the angle of the curve leading up to each point as you press will ensure the cloth hugs the pattern piece, and the finished point will be crisp and precise.

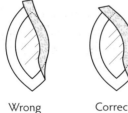

Wrong   Correct!

3. To prepare an inner point or pronounced inner curve, stop pressing the seam allowance just shy of the center clipped section. Reaching under the appliqué at the clip, use the pad of your finger to smooth the clipped section of fabric snugly onto the paper, following immediately behind with the iron in a sweeping motion to fuse the fibers in place onto the paper.

Always turn your prepared appliqué over to the front to evaluate your pressing and adjust any areas that could be improved. Tiny imperfections can be smoothed by nudging them with the point of your hot iron, and more pronounced imperfections can be loosened and re-pressed from the back.

Making Bias-Tube Stems and Vines

To achieve finished stems and vines that can be curved flawlessly and don't require the seam allowances to be turned under, I use bias tubes. After cutting the strips specified in the project instructions (and referring to "Cutting Bias Strips" on page 96 for guidelines), prepare them as follows:

1. With *wrong* sides together, fold the strip in half lengthwise and stitch a scant ¼" from the long raw edges to form a tube. (I stitch my seams about two or three threads less than a true ¼", as this often eliminates the need to trim the seam allowances and allows the bias bar to slide through the sewn fabric tube more easily.) For any stem sewn from a strip with a cut width of 1" or less, you'll likely need to trim the seam allowances to approximately ⅛" so they will be hidden when the stem is viewed from the front.

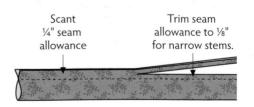

Scant ¼" seam allowance

Trim seam allowance to ⅛" for narrow stems.

2. Because seam allowance differences can occur, the best bias-bar width for each project can vary from person to person, even for stems of the same size. Ultimately, I've found it's best to simply choose a bar that will fit comfortably into the sewn tube, and then slide it along as you press the stem flat to one side, centering the seam allowances so they won't be visible from the front.

Bias bar

3. Remove the bias bar and place small dots of liquid basting glue at approximately ½" to 1" intervals along the seam line underneath the layers of the pressed seam allowances; use a hot, dry iron on the wrong side of the stem, allowing it to rest on each area of the stem for two or three seconds, to heat set the glue and fuse the seam allowances in place.

Basting Appliqués

Invisible machine appliqué, like traditional hand appliqué, is sewn in layers from the bottom to the top. Keep in mind as you lay out and baste your appliqués that it's a good practice to leave approximately ½" between the outermost appliqués of your design and the raw edge of your background because this will preserve an intact margin of space around each piece after the quilt top has been assembled.

1. Lay out the prepared appliqués on the background to ensure that everything fits and is to your liking. As you lay out your pieces, remember that any appliqué with a raw edge that will be overlapped by another piece (such as a stem) should be overlapped by approximately ¼" to prevent fraying.

2. Remove all but the bottom appliqués and baste them in place. Liquid basting glue for fabric is my preferred basting method because there are no pins to stitch around or remove and the appliqués will not shift or cause the background cloth to shrink as they're stitched. I suggest glue basting your appliqués as follows:

Without shifting the appliqué from its position, fold over one half of the shape to expose the back and place small dots of liquid basting glue along the fabric seam allowances (not the freezer-paper pattern piece) at approximately ½" to 1" intervals. Firmly push the glue-basted portion of the appliqué in place with your hand and repeat with the remaining half of the shape. From the back, use a hot, dry iron to heat set the glue.

Preparing Your Sewing Machine

Monofilament thread produces results that are nearly invisible and it's easy to use once you know how to prepare your sewing machine. Be sure to match your monofilament thread to your appliqué, not your background, choosing the smoke color for medium and dark prints and clear for bright colors and pastels. If you're not sure which color is the best choice, lay a strand of each thread over your print to audition them. Whenever possible, use the upright spool pin position on your sewing machine for the monofilament, as this will facilitate a smooth, even feed.

1. Use a size 75/11 (or smaller) machine-quilting needle in your sewing machine and thread it with monofilament. I've discovered that prints with a subtle texture, and often batiks, can make needle holes more visible, so if this occurs, I recommend substituting a smaller needle.

2. Wind the bobbin with all-purpose, neutral-colored thread. In my experience, a 50-weight (or heavier) thread works well for this technique in most sewing machines, as it will resist sliding through the cloth and pulling up through the surface of your appliqués. Also, keep in mind that prewound bobbins, while convenient, can sometimes make it difficult to achieve perfectly balanced tension for this technique.

   Note: If your machine's bobbin case features a "finger" with a special eye for use with embroidery techniques, threading your bobbin thread through this opening will often provide additional tension control to perfectly regulate your stitches.

Sturdy Bobbin Thread for Invisible Results

It may seem counterintuitive to use a very sturdy thread in the bobbin in combination with the fine monofilament thread in your needle, but after observing the results achieved with a variety of sewing machines in numerous workshops that I've taught, I've discovered that fine-gauge threads can often pull up through the surface of the appliqué and leave visible dots along edges of the stitched shapes. If the thread you're using is very fine and continues to be visible, even after adjusting the tension level of your sewing machine, try using a 50-weight thread. If the thread dots still remain visible, consider experimenting with an even heavier thread, as it will resist pulling up through the surface and remain on the underside of the appliqué for truly invisible results.

3. Program your sewing machine to the zigzag stitch, adjust the width and length to achieve a tiny stitch as shown below (keeping in mind that your inner stitches should land two or three threads inside your appliqué, with your outer stitches piercing the background immediately next to the appliqué), and reduce the tension setting. For many sewing machines, a width, length, and tension setting of 1 produces the perfect stitch.

Approximate stitch size

Stitching Appliqués

Before stitching your first invisible machine appliqué project, I recommend experimenting with a simple pattern shape to become comfortable with this technique and find the best settings for your sewing machine. Keep your test piece as a quick reference for future projects, making a note directly on the background fabric as to your machine's width, length, and tension settings, and even whether your machine begins zigzag stitching on the left or the right. Also, if you routinely use more than one type of thread in your bobbin, you should make a note of the thread that was used for your test piece—if the thread in your bobbin is changed for a different type, the balance of your components may change as well, and your settings may need to be adjusted.

1. Slide the basted appliqué under the sewing-machine needle from front to back to direct the threads behind the machine, positioning a straight or gently curved edge under the needle.

2. Place your fingertip over the monofilament tail or grasp the threads as your machine takes two or three stitches. Release the threads and continue zigzag stitching around your shape, with your inner stitches landing on the appliqué and your outer stitches piercing the background immediately next to the appliqué. Train your eyes to watch the outer stitches while you sew to keep your appliqué positioned correctly and the inner stitches will naturally fall into place. After a short distance, pause and carefully clip the monofilament tail close to the background.

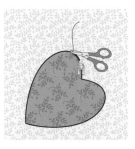

To maintain good control as you work your way around each shape, stitch your appliqué at a slow to moderate speed, stopping and pivoting as often as needed to keep the edge of your shape feeding straight toward the needle, with the appliqué positioned to the left of the needle, as you would for patchwork. Whenever possible, pivot with the needle down inside the appliqué, because the paper pattern piece will stabilize the shape and prevent it from stretching or becoming distorted.

- If dots of bobbin thread appear along the top surface edge of your appliqué as you stitch, further adjust the tension settings on your machine (usually lower) until they disappear.

- Your machine's stitch should look like a true zigzag pattern on the wrong side of your work. If the monofilament thread is visible underneath your appliqué from the back, or the stitches appear loose or loopy, adjust the tension settings (usually higher) until they're secure.

3. To firmly secure an inner appliqué point, stitch to the position where the inner stitch rests exactly on the inner point of the appliqué and stop. Pivot the fabric, and with the appliqué inner point at a right angle to the needle, continue stitching. For pieces with inner points that seem delicate, I often pivot and stitch this area twice to secure it well.

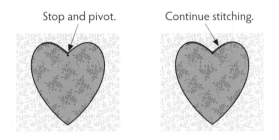

Stop and pivot.   Continue stitching.

4. To secure an outer point, stitch to the position where the outer stitch lands exactly next to the appliqué point in the background and stop. Pivot the fabric and continue stitching along the next side of the shape. As you begin sewing again, a second stitch will drop into the point of the appliqué.

Stop and pivot.   Continue stitching.

5. Continue stitching around the edge of the appliqué until you overlap your starting point by approximately ¼". End with a locking stitch if your machine offers this feature, placing it on either the appliqué or the background, wherever it will best be hidden. For machines without a locking stitch, extend your overlapped area to about ½" and your appliqué will remain well secured.

I've discovered that using a locking stitch to finish each appliqué doesn't make your stitching more secure, it simply communicates to your sewing machine that you've finished your current task, enabling you to easily position your next piece for stitching because the needle will consistently align and begin in the same position.

6. From time to time, it's a good practice to evaluate your stitch placement along your appliqué edges to ensure you're achieving the best possible results. To do this, hold a completed appliqué piece up to the light and view it with the light shining from behind. A properly stitched appliqué will have a ring of tiny needle holes encircling the appliqué in the background cloth. If your results appear different, then adjustments to the placement of your work under the needle should be made as you stitch future pieces.

String Appliqué

When two or more appliqués are in close proximity on the same layer, I recommend stitching your first appliqué as instructed in "Stitching Appliqués" on page 104, but instead of clipping the threads when you finish, lift the presser foot and slide the background to the next appliqué without lifting it from the sewing-machine surface. Lower the presser foot and resume stitching the next appliqué, remembering to end with a locking stitch or overlap your starting position by ¼" to ½". After the cluster of appliqués has been stitched, carefully clip the threads between each.

Removing Paper Pattern Pieces

On the wrong side of the stitched appliqué, use embroidery scissors to carefully pinch and cut through the fabric at least ¼" inside the appliqué seam. Trim away the background fabric, leaving a generous ¼" seam allowance. Grasp the appliqué edge between the thumb and forefinger of one hand, and grab the seam allowances immediately opposite with the other hand. Give a gentle but firm tug to free the paper edge. Next, use your fingertip to loosen the glue anchoring the pattern piece to the fabric; peel away and discard the paper. Any paper that remains in the appliqué corners can be pulled out with a pair of tweezers. Please rest easy that cutting away the fabric behind an appliqué won't weaken the quilt top in any way—this method of stitching is very secure, and it will enable designs with multiple layers to remain soft and pliable, without any stiff or bulky areas.

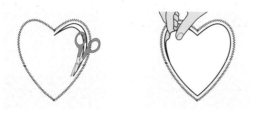

Completing the Machine-Appliqué Process

Working from the bottom layer to the top, continue basting and stitching the appliqués until each one has been secured in place, remembering to remove the paper pattern pieces before adding each new layer. Keep in mind that it isn't necessary to stitch any edge that will be overlapped by another piece. If needed, *briefly* press your finished work from the back to ensure the seam allowances lie smooth and flat. Always take care not to apply direct heat to the front of your appliqués, as this could weaken the monofilament threads.

Wool Appliqué

Wool is a really fun, fast, and forgiving fabric to work with, and I especially love the magic that happens when it's used in combination with traditional cotton fabrics. Wool that's been felted has a soft, densely woven feel to the cloth and it resists raveling as you work with it. I suggest that you use only 100% wool and, as a general rule, avoid worsted wool because it doesn't felt well and can be challenging to work with. You can usually identify worsted wool by its hard, flat weave, and you'll often find it used for garments such as men's suits.

For my method of appliquéing with wool, you'll need the following items in addition to your standard quiltmaking supplies:

- #8 or #12 perle cotton in colors to match or complement your wool
- Embroidery needle (a size 5 works well for me)
- Freezer paper
- Liquid basting glue, water-soluble and acid-free (my favorite brand is Quilter's Choice Basting Glue by Beacon Adhesives)
- Paper-backed fusible web (I like the results achieved when using HeatnBond Lite)
- Sharp scissors with a fine point
- Thimble

Felting Your Wool

If your wool hasn't been felted, this is easy to do. Wash similar-hued wool pieces in the washing machine on the longest cycle using a hot-water wash and a cold-water rinse. (You may wish to skim the surface of the water once or twice during the cycle to prevent loose fibers from clogging the drain.) Next, dry the wool in your dryer, again using the longest and hottest setting. Remove the dry wool promptly to help prevent wrinkles from forming.

As an added safety measure, I always wash and dry vividly colored pieces separately when I suspect they might lose dye, and I never wash wool that has been over dyed, since it will almost certainly bleed color—if I'm not sure whether a piece has been over dyed, I follow the rule that it's better to be safe and ask rather than to guess and be sorry. Finally, never wash wool that's been included as part of a kitted project, because it can continue to shrink and you may find yourself without enough wool to complete your design.

Preparing Wool Appliqués

When working with wool, I like to use a fusible appliqué technique for the preparation steps, liquid basting glue for basting the layers of wool together, and perle cotton and an embroidery needle as I stitch the pieces. The combination of the fusible adhesive and the liquid glue produces ideal results because the iron-on adhesive finishes and stabilizes the underside of the wool edges to reduce fraying, while the glue-basted edges hold the layers of wool together beautifully for easy stitching without pinning.

Keep in mind when you're using the following technique that your finished wool shapes will appear backward and be reversed on your quilt if they are directional and aren't perfectly symmetrical.

1. Trace each appliqué shape the number of times indicated in the pattern instructions onto the paper side of your iron-on adhesive, leaving approximately ½" between each shape. For projects with numerous identical shapes (or nonsymmetrical shapes that need to be reversed), make a template as instructed in "Preparing Pattern Templates" on page 100 and use it to trace the required number of pieces. Remember that for this method you'll need one traced iron-on adhesive shape for each appliqué.

2. Cut out each shape approximately ¼" *outside* the drawn lines, and then cut away the center portion of the shape approximately ¼" *inside* the drawn lines to eliminate bulk and keep the shape pliable after the appliqué has been stitched. For added stability in large shapes, leave a narrow strip of paper across the middle of the shape as you cut away the excess center portion, because this will act as a bridge to connect the sides and prevent distortion as you lay out your shape onto the wool.

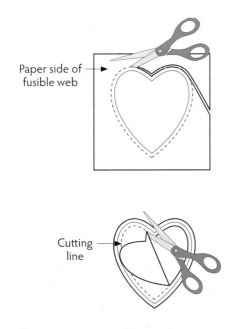

Paper side of fusible web

Cutting line

3. Following the manufacturer's instructions, fuse each shape, paper side *up*, to the *wrong* side of the fabric. After the fabric has cooled, cut out each shape exactly on the drawn lines. To protect the fusible adhesive and prevent the fabric appliqué edges from fraying, I suggest leaving the paper backing on your prepared pieces until you're ready to use them. To easily remove the paper backing, loosen an inside edge of the paper with a needle and peel it away.

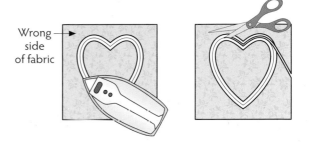

Wrong side of fabric

Stitching Wool Appliqués

After much experimenting, I've decided that the overhand stitch is my preferred method of appliquéing wool shapes because it's quick, uses less thread, provides a softer look than the blanket stitch, and the stitches stay in place without rolling over the appliqué edge.

Whenever possible, I work from the top layer to the bottom to stitch any layered wool pieces into units (such as a stack of pennies) *before* adding them to my background, because this simplifies the sewing process and eliminates the need to stitch through multiple heavy layers of wool. Once the layered units have been sewn together, the appliqué designs can be stitched to the background, working from the bottom layer to the top.

1. Lay out your appliqués, including any stitched appliqué units, onto your background to ensure everything fits and is to your liking. Remove all but the bottom pieces, remove the paper backing on each remaining piece, and glue baste them in place, referring to "Basting Appliqués" on page 103 and applying small dots of liquid glue directly onto the narrow margin of fusible adhesive that rims each shape.

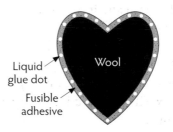

Liquid glue dot

Wool

Fusible adhesive

2. Use an embroidery needle threaded with a single knotted strand of #8 or #12 perle cotton to overhand stitch the pieces in place as shown below.

Overhand stitch

3. Lay out, remove the paper backing, baste, and stitch the next layer of appliqués, ensuring that any appliqué overlapping another piece does so by at least ¼". Continue working from the bottom layer to the top to complete the appliqué design, keeping in mind that it isn't necessary to cut away the backs of any appliqués stitched from wool.

Completing the Quilt Top

Once the individual components of your quilt have been finished, assembling everything and adding your borders is the next step. The information that follows will help simplify and streamline this process.

Assembling the Quilt Center

Lay out your blocks or units, evaluating their placement and making any necessary changes; I suggest positioning blocks or units with strong hues into your corners to visually anchor and define the quilt center.

For greater ease when assembling large tops, join the rows in groups of two or three. Next, join the grouped rows, working from the top and bottom edges toward the middle until you join all the rows.

Adding Borders

When joining border strips to the center of a quilt, fold each border piece in half to find the midpoint, and then finger-press a crease. Next fold each side of the quilt center in half and crease these midpoint positions as well. Align the creases of your individual components and pin them together for a perfect fit.

All of the measurements provided in this book for whole cloth borders are mathematically correct, but because there is little or no stretch to these pieces when they've been cut from the lengthwise grain, you may wish to slightly increase the designated lengths.

I routinely increase the length of my strips by ½" for borders measuring up to 60" long and by 1" for strips in excess of 60"; any excess length can be trimmed away after the borders are added.

Finishing Techniques

There are many choices available as you work through the final steps of your project—tailoring these decisions to suit your individual preferences will result in a finished quilt that reflects your own unique tastes and personality.

Batting

For quilt tops sewn from prewashed fabrics, I suggest using polyester batting, or a cotton/polyester blend, because it will ensure minimal shrinkage when your quilt is laundered. If your quilt top was stitched from fabrics that weren't prewashed, I'd recommend choosing cotton batting, particularly if you love the slightly puckered look of vintage quilts. Regardless of your choice, always follow the manufacturer's instructions for the very best results.

Backing

I cut and piece my quilt backings to be approximately 3"–5" larger than my quilt top on all sides. As you consider your backing fabric choices, remember that prints with a lot of texture will make your quilting less visible, while muted prints and solids will emphasize your quilting design. To prevent shadowing, use fabrics in colors similar to those in your quilt top.

For the best use of your yardage, I suggest seaming your quilt backings as shown.

Lap quilts
up to 74" square

Twin-size bed quilts
up to 74" wide

Full- and queen-size bed
quilts up to 90" wide

King-size bed quilts
up to 107" wide

Basting

To prepare your finished top for the quilting process:

1. Place the backing fabric, wrong side up, on a large, flat surface. Smooth away any wrinkles and secure the edges with masking tape.

2. Center the batting on the backing fabric and smooth away any wrinkles.

3. Carefully center the quilt top on the layered batting and backing. For hand quilting, use white thread to baste diagonally from corner to corner, and then at 3" to 4" intervals as shown. For machine quilting, pin baste using size 2 rustproof safety pins and working from the center outward at 4" to 5" intervals as shown. Last, thread baste the edges.

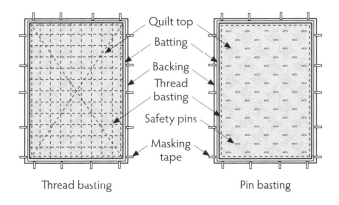

Thread basting   Pin basting

Marking Quilting Designs

A quick and easy way to mark straight quilting lines is to use painter's low-adhesive masking tape in various widths as a stitching guide, but always remember to remove the tape at the end of each day to prevent adhesive from damaging your fabric. More elaborate designs can be marked onto the top using a quilter's pencil or a fine-tipped water-soluble marker—doing this before the layers are assembled will provide a smooth marking surface and produce the best results. For a beautiful finish, always ensure your quilt features an abundant and evenly spaced amount of quilting.

Hand Quilting

To hand quilt your project, place the layered quilt top in a hoop or frame and follow these steps:

1. Thread your needle with an approximately 18" length of quilting thread and knot one end. Insert the needle into the quilt top about 1" from where you wish to begin quilting, sliding it through the layers and bringing it up through the

top; gently tug until the knot is drawn down into the layer of batting.

2. Sew small, even stitches through the layers until you near the end of the thread. Make a knot in the thread about 1/8" from the quilt top. Insert and slide the needle through the batting layer, bringing it back up about 1" beyond your last stitch, tugging gently until the knot disappears; carefully clip the thread.

Hand-quilting stitch

Big-Stitch Quilting

Big-stitch quilting (sometimes called "utility stitch") is one of my favorite methods because it's a quick way to include hand stitching on my projects without the huge time commitment that traditional hand quilting can require. For this style of quilting I use a size 5 embroidery needle and #8 or #12 perle cotton to sew a running stitch (with each stitch approximately 1/8" to a scant 1/4" long) through the quilt layers, ending my stitches as I would for traditional hand quilting.

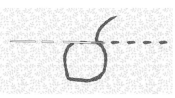

Machine Quilting

For in-depth machine-quilting instructions, please refer to *You Can Quilt It!* by Deborah Poole (Martingale, 2014).

When an overall style of quilting is my best choice to add subtle texture without introducing another design element into my project mix, I use a swirling pattern.

To stitch this versatile design, sew a free-form circle of any size, and then fill in the center with ever-reducing concentric circles (think cinnamon rolls). When you arrive at the center, stitch a gently curved line to the next area to be swirled and continue filling the block or top, staggering the placement and size of the swirls, until the stitching is complete.

Start here.

Binding

Traditionally, a 2½"-wide French-fold binding is used to finish most quilts. When I bind my quilts, however, I prefer a more unconventional method using 2"-wide strips that result in a traditional look from the front while producing a "chubby" border of color to frame the backing in a more striking manner. The binding yardage for each project will accommodate either method, with enough binding to encircle the quilt perimeter plus approximately 10" for mitered corners.

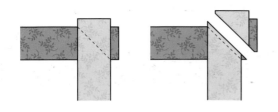

Traditional French-fold binding   Chubby binding

Traditional French-Fold Binding

1. With right sides together, join the 2½"-wide strips end to end at right angles, stitching diagonally across the corners, to make one long strip. Trim the seam allowances to ¼" and press them open.

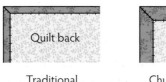

2. Cut one end at a 45° angle and press it under ¼". Fold the strip in half lengthwise with wrong sides together, and press.

Fold line

3. Beginning along one side of the quilt top, not at a corner, use a ¼" seam allowance to stitch the binding along the raw edges. Stop sewing ¼" from the first corner and backstitch. Clip the thread and remove the quilt from under the presser foot.

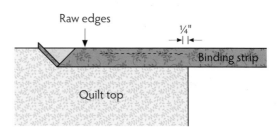

Raw edges

¼"

Binding strip

Quilt top

4. Make a fold in the binding, bringing it up and back down onto itself to square the corner. Rotate the quilt 90° and reposition it under the presser foot. Resume sewing at the top edge of the quilt, continuing around the perimeter in this manner.

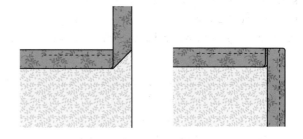

5. When you approach your starting point, cut the binding end at an angle 1" longer than needed and tuck it inside the previously sewn binding to enclose the raw end. Complete the stitching.

6. Bring the folded edge of the binding to the back of the quilt, enclosing the raw edges. Use a blind stitch and matching thread to hand sew the binding to the back. At each corner, fold the binding to form a miter and hand stitch it in place.

Securely Stitched Binding

When I'm hand stitching my binding and come to the end of my length of thread, I tie a double knot before sliding my needle between the quilt layers to bury the thread tail and keep it hidden without pulling up to the surface. When I rethread and continue stitching, I begin my new stitches about 1" behind the point where I previously finished, so that there is an overlapped area. This small overlapped section of stitching reinforces and strengthens my starting and stopping points to help them stay secure, and I never need to worry that my binding will become loose as my quilt is used.

Chubby Binding

For this method, you'll need a bias-tape maker designed to produce 1"-wide, double-fold tape. For most of my quilts, I prefer to use binding strips that have been cut on the straight of grain, rather than the bias, because I feel this gives my quilt edges added stability. For scrappy bindings pieced from many prints of different lengths, I join the strips end to end using straight seams and start with a straight fold at the beginning.

1. Cut the strips 2" wide and join them end to end. Next, slide the pieced strip through the bias-tape maker, pressing the folds with a hot, dry iron as they emerge so the raw edges meet in the center. As the tape maker slides along the pieced strip, the seams will automatically be directed to one side as they are pressed.

2. Open the fold of the strip along the top edge only. Turn the beginning raw end under ½" and

finger-press the fold. Starting along one side of the quilt top, not at a corner, align the unfolded raw edge of the binding with the raw edge of the quilt and stitch as instructed in steps 3 and 4 of the French-fold method as previously instructed.

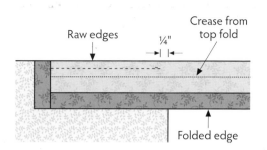

Raw edges | ¼" | Crease from top fold | Folded edge

3. When you approach your starting point, cut the end to extend 1" beyond the folded edge and complete the stitching.

4. Bring the wide folded edge of the binding to the back and hand stitch it (including the mitered folds at the corners) as instructed in step 6 of the French-fold method. The raw end of the strip will now be encased within the binding.

Attaching a Quilt Label

To document your work, remember to prepare a fabric quilt label including any information you'd like to share, and then hand stitch it to the back of your quilt.

Personalized Quilt Labels

My friend Barb Stommel told me about a really creative idea for personalizing her quilt labels, and it's so clever that I'd love to share it with you. Barb prepares her labels using the Printed Treasures fabric sheets by Miliken, created for use with inkjet printers, and includes a photo of herself along with the information she wishes to share about her quilt. This one-of-a-kind picture label adds a truly personal touch for future generations who will use and enjoy her labor of love through the years.

About the Author

After falling in love with a sampler quilt pattern in the late 1990s, Kim taught herself the steps needed to make it, and was forever hooked on quiltmaking. Her second quilt was of her own original design and with her third quilt, she became the winner of *American Patchwork & Quilting* magazine's 1998 Pieces of the Past quilt challenge, turning her life down a whole new and unexpected path. Kim's very favorite quilts have always been those sewn from simple tried-and-true patchwork designs, especially when combined with appliqué, and she loves designing and stitching these traditionally inspired quilts using modern techniques for the perfect blend of simplicity and charm.

Since 1998, Kim's work has been featured in numerous national and international quilting magazines including *American Patchwork & Quilting*, *Love of Quilting*, *Primitive Quilts and Projects*, *McCall's Quick Quilts*, *Australian Homespun*, and *Australian Quilter's Companion*. Her easy quiltmaking and invisible machine appliqué techniques led to an extensive teaching and travel schedule for several years, and Kim is slowly beginning to whittle down her days away from home as her husband nears retirement.

In addition to teaching her methods and authoring her "Simple" series of books with Martingale, Kim continues to design fabric collections for Henry Glass & Co., enabling her to be involved in the full circle of quiltmaking from start to finish—what a wonderful experience for a girl who began her journey wondering if she had what it took to make a single quilt!

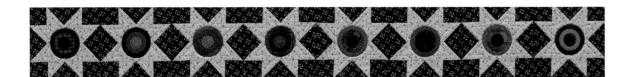